Red Books *showing the way*

LOCAL STREET ATLAS

CORBY · KETTER
WELLINGBOROUGH

BURTON LATIMER · DESBOROUGH · MARKET HARBOROUGH
RAUNDS · ROTHWELL · RUSHDEN · WELDON · WOLLASTON

CONTENTS

Legend:

- Pedestrianized / Restricted Access
- Track
- Built Up Area
- Footpath
- Stream
- River
- Lock — Canal
- Railway / Station
- ● Post Office
- P — Car Park / Park & Ride
- C Public Convenience
- + Place of Worship
- → One-way Street
- *i* Tourist Information Centre
- ▲8 ▲8 Adjoining Pages
- Area Depicting Enlarged Centre
- Emergency Services
- Industrial Buildings
- Leisure Buildings
- Education Buildings
- Hotels etc.
- Retail Buildings
- General Buildings
- Woodland
- Orchard
- Recreational / Parkland
- Cemetery

Every effort has been made to verify the accuracy of information in this book but the publishers cannot accept responsibility for expense or loss caused by an error or omission.

Information that will be of assistance to the user of the maps will be welcomed.

The representation on these maps of a road, track or path is no evidence of the existence of a right of way.

Street plans prepared and published by Red Books (Estate Publications) Ltd, Bridewell House, Tenterden, Kent. The Publishers acknowledge the co-operation of the local authorities of towns represented in this atlas.

Ordnance Survey® This product includes mapping data licensed from Ordnance Survey® with the permission of the Controller of Her Majesty's Stationery Office.

www.redbooks-maps.co.uk

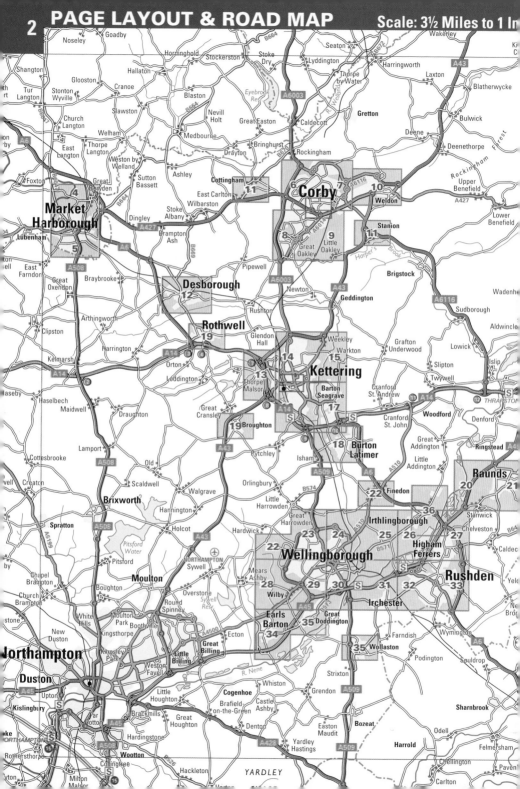

CORBY ENLARGED CENTRE

Scale: 7 Inches to 1 Mile

KETTERING ENLARGED CENTRE

Scale: 7 Inches to 1 Mile

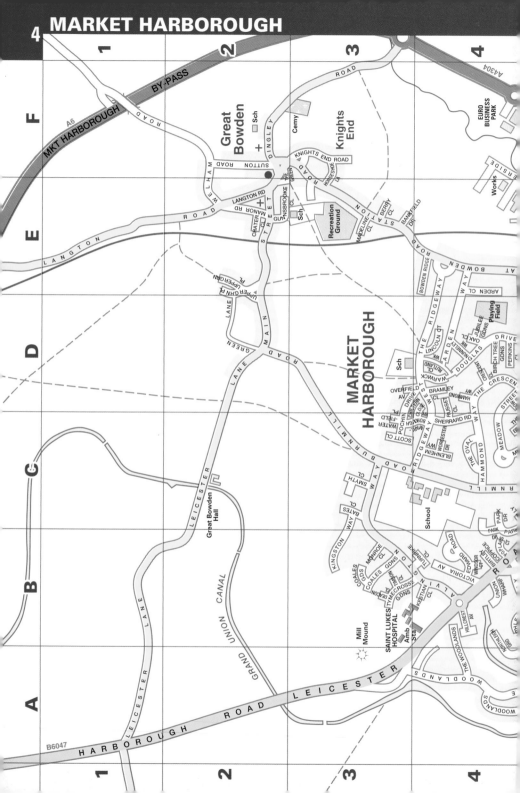

MARKET HARBOROUGH

4

1 · 2 · 3 · 4

F
E
D
C
B
A

MKT HARBOROUGH BY-PASS

A6

ROAD

Great Bowden

Sch

Cemy

KNIGHTS END ROAD

Knights End

ROAD

EURO BUSINESS PARK

Works

DINGLEY

SUTTON ROAD

THE GREEN

HORSESHOE LA

STATION ROAD

BERRY CL

BANKFIELD DR

BOWDEN

ROAD

ARDEN CL

WELHAM ROAD

LANGTON ROAD

LANGTON RD

MANOR RD

CHATER CL

GUNSBROKE CL

Sch

Recreation Ground

MADELINE CL

BOWDEN RIDGE

THE RIDGEWAY

RIDGEWAY

WAY

JUBILEE GDNS

Playing Field

OAK CL

UPPER GRN PL

UPPER GRN PL

GREEN LANE

MAIN STREET

ROAD

MARKET HARBOROUGH

Sch

OVERFIELD AV

WATER-FIELD RD

BOROUGH

CHILDERS CLOSE

DRIVE

BRAMLEY

CLOSE

RUSSEL CL

WORCESTER

LINCOLN CT

WARWICK GDNS

RUTLAND

HAMMOND

DOUGLAS GDNS

BIRCH TREE GDNS

PERKINS DRIVE

THE CRESCENT

STREET

THE OVAL

MEADOW

BLENHEIM WY

SHERRARD RD

BURNMILL ROAD

HAMMOND

RNMLL

Leicester Lane

Great Bowden Hall

LEICESTER LANE

GRAND UNION CANAL

KINGSTON AVM

SMYTH CL

BATES CL

School

MONROE CL

COALES GDNS

COALES CL

TY MECROSS

ALVINGTON GDNS

DEMON

KESTIAN AV

TURNELL CL

VICTORIA AV

ROAD

BENTLEY AV

TOPFIELD

WINWARD

WARD RD

ALVINGTON WAY

HILLCREST AV

PARK DR

PARK

PARK

WHARF

THE WOODLANDS

WOODLANDS

Mill Mound

SAINT LUKES HOSPITAL

Amb Sta

HARBOROUGH ROAD LEICESTER

B6047

1 · 2 · 3 · 4

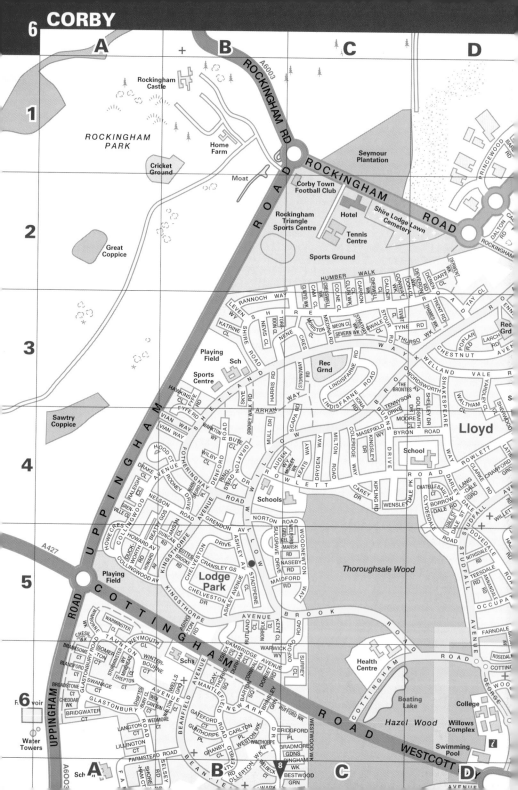

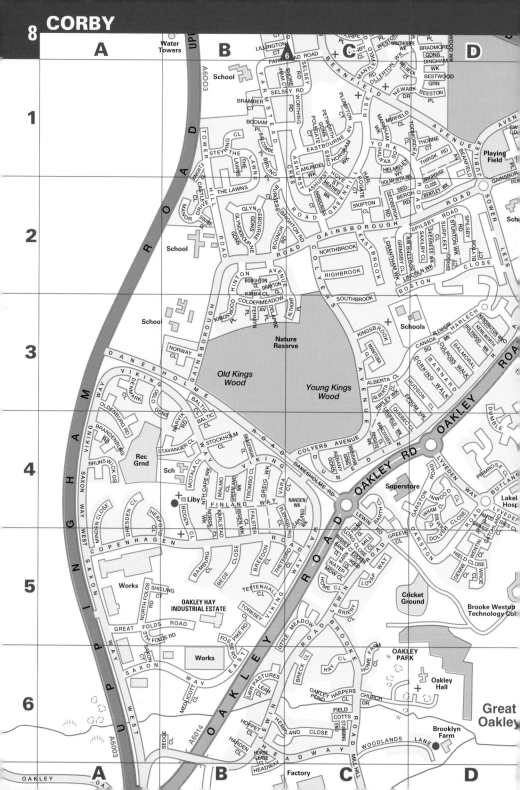

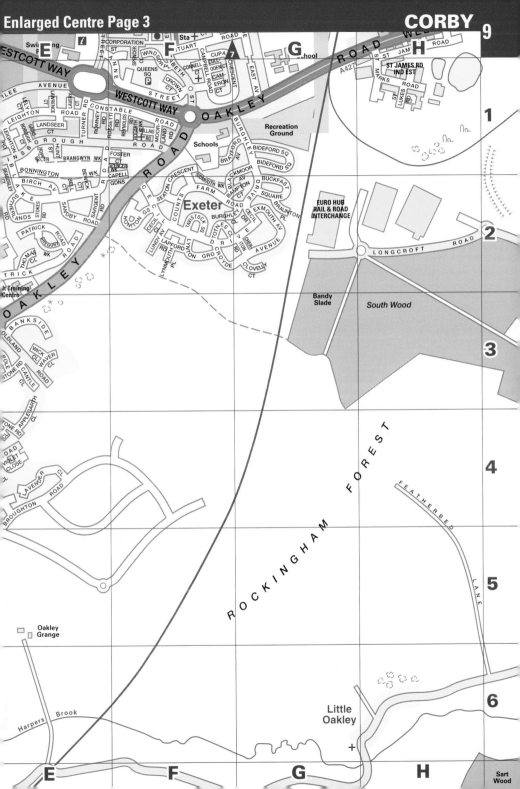

ESTCOTT WAY

E

Swi ng
Po

i

CORPORATION

Sta

ROAD

STUART

ROAD WE H ROAD

CORBY
9

F

QUEENS
SQ
P
CROWN
CT

WINDSOR

SPENCER

ABETH
ST
ANNE
CAMPBELL ROAD
CT
EAST
AV

G
School
CUPA
CRESCENT
CAM-
ERON
CT

A427
ST JAMS
ST
MARKS

ST
ROAD
ST JAMES RD
IND EST
LUKES RD
LUKES

CONNELL RD
ODEN
CT

DULL-

WESTCOTT WAY

LEIGHTON
ROAD

AVENUE

LAWRENCE
CT

CONSTABLE
RD

ROAD OAKLEY

OAKLEY

Recreation
Ground

1

LANDSEER
CT

TURNER RD

REYNOLDS
RD

MOOR

BURGHLEY

BIDEFORD SQ

LANDSEER

LEIGHTON
RD

GINS
RD

BONWICK

ROMNEY
RD

ROSSETTI
RD

MILLAIS
RD

ELIZABETH
RD

Schools

BRAFORD

BIDEFORD SQ

BOROUGH
ROAD

HUNT
ST

BRANGWYN WK

FOSTER
CT

SIDMOUTH WK

BLACKMOOR
AV

BUCKFAST

BONNINGTON

BIRCH AV

BELL
CT

BEWICK

SPENCER
WK

CAPELL
GDNS

FARM

BAMPTON
DRIVE

BRAUNTON
PL

SQUARE

PATRICK

SARGENT
RD

SANDBY ROAD

Exeter

SEATON CRESCENT

TAVISTOCK RD

EXMOUTH AV

EURO HUB
RAIL & ROAD
INTERCHANGE

2

THOMAS
CL

GREGORY
WK

CECIL

HINTON GS

CECIL

COUNTS

TOTNES CT

BURGHLEY
DR

CECIL

LONGCROFT ROAD

TRICK

It Training
Centre

LUNDY AV

LAPFORD
RD

LYNTON

GROVE

CLOVELLY
CT

Bandy
Slade

South Wood

3

BANKSIDE

OLDLAND

WICK
CL

WAVER
CL

CANTLE
ROAD

OAKLEY

R O C K I N G H A M   F O R E S T

F
E
A
T
H
E
R
B
E
D

ONE RD

POLE

APPLEGARTH
CL

VIOLET
CLOSE

4

LAVENDER

CT

ROAD

BROUGHTON

5

L
A
N
E

Oakley
Grange

Harpers

Brook

Little
Oakley

6

Sart
Wood

E   F   G   H

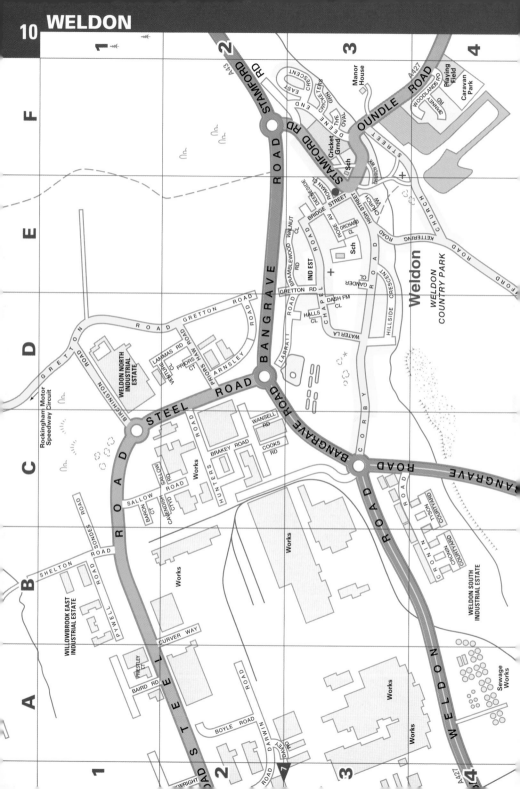

WELDON

WELDON COUNTRY PARK

WELDON NORTH INDUSTRIAL ESTATE

WELDON SOUTH INDUSTRIAL ESTATE

WILLOWBROOK EAST INDUSTRIAL ESTATE

Rockingham Motor Speedway Circuit

STAMFORD ROAD

STAMFORD RD

BANGRAVE ROAD

STEEL ROAD

BANGRAVE ROAD

GRETTON ROAD

BIRCHINGTON ROAD

OUNDLE ROAD

CHURCH ROAD

KETTERING ROAD

CORBY ROAD

WELDON ROAD

Manor House

Playing Field

Caravan Park

Cricket Grnd

IND EST

DASH FM

Sewage Works

Works

Works

Works

Works

Works

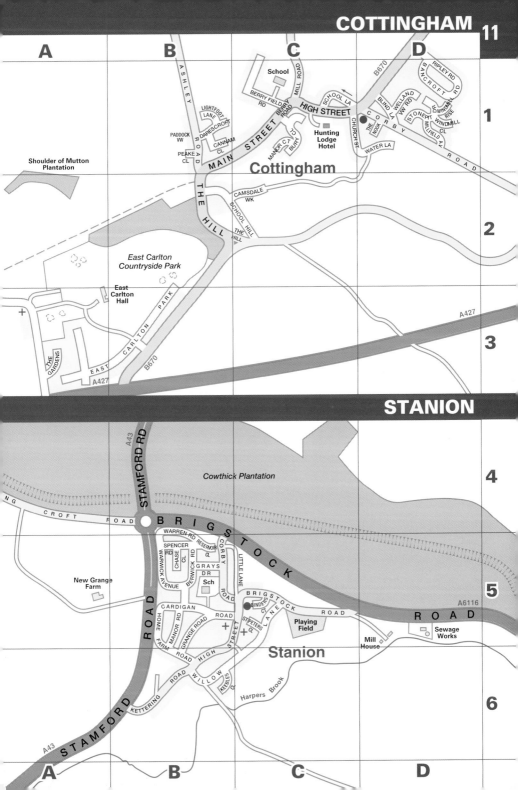

COTTINGHAM (map panel)

- A B C D — grid columns 1, 2, 3
- Shoulder of Mutton Plantation
- School
- ASHLEY ROAD
- LIGHTFOOT LANE
- PADDOCK VW
- DARESCROFT
- PEAKE CL
- CANNAM CL
- MANOR CT
- BERRY FIELDS RD
- BERRY RD
- MILL ROAD
- SCHOOL LA
- HIGH STREET
- Hunting Lodge Hotel
- BURY
- Cottingham
- MAIN STREET ROAD
- THE HILL
- CAMSDALE WK
- SCHOOL HILL
- THE HILL
- CHURCH ST
- WATER LA
- THE NOOK
- THE CORBY
- COOBY
- BLIND LA
- WELLAND VW
- WELLAND RD
- STONEBY RD
- MILLFIELD CL
- WINDMILL CL
- WINDMILL RISE
- WINDMILL AV
- BANCROFT RD
- RIPLEY RD
- B670
- ROAD
- East Carlton Countryside Park
- East Carlton Hall
- CARLTON PARK
- EAST
- THE GARDENS
- B670
- A427
- A427

STANION (map panel)

- A43
- STAMFORD RD
- Cowthick Plantation
- NG
- CROFT ROAD
- WARREN RD
- RESERVOIR RD
- SPENCER RD
- WARWICK AVENUE
- CHASE CL
- BERWICK RD
- GRAYS DR
- CORBY ROAD
- BRIGSTOCK
- LITTLE LANE
- New Grange Farm
- Sch
- CARDIGAN
- HOME FARM ROAD
- MANOR RD
- GRANGE ROAD
- ROAD
- BINDERS CT
- BRIGSTOCK LANE
- ST PETERS CL
- HIGH STREET
- KEEBLES CL
- WILLOW ROAD
- KETTERING ROAD
- Playing Field
- ROAD
- A6116
- ROAD
- Sewage Works
- Mill House
- Harpers Brook
- Stanion
- STAMFORD ROAD
- A43

Gaultney Wood

WATERMILL CL

THE OSIERS

SYCAMORE DR

Cemy

WILLOW

EASTBROOK

AUBE

REDWOOD RD

BRADLAW

THE HAWTHORNS

Leisure Centre

CHESTNUT DR

Playing Field

COPELANDS ROAD

HEREFORD CL

WESTMORLAND DRIVE

MAYFIELD RD

FURLONG RD

AVENUE

WILLOW CT

RUSHTON

LEYS

AVENUE

CEDAR

PINE CL

VALLEY RISE

HEADLANDS

ISE VALE AVENUE

VALLEY RISE

BROOKSIDE

ISE VIEW ROAD

PRINCES AV

BREAKLEYS

ROAD

CHERRY TREE CL

FOXLANDS

REGENT STREET

QUEEN STREET

Fire Sta

CHURCH VIEW ROAD

VALLEY ROAD

MILLHOLME

KENMORE DR

RUSHTON ROAD

KING STREET

Schs

CHAPLINS LANE

Recreation Ground

ROMAN WAY

WILTON CL

UPPER STEEPING

ROMAN WAY

LOWERING

UNION STREET

PIPE WELL

BURLEY CL

HAVELOCK ST

NEW ST

NICHOLS STREET

GLADSTONE ST

MAYFIELD

WELLAND

PADDOCK CL

ST GILES CL

DUNKIRK

BEECH CL

GOLD STREET

STATION

VICTORIA ST

SAXON ST

Lbry

HIGH STREET

LOWER ST

River Ise

ROAD

RO

ROTHWELL

Desborough

STOKE ROAD

B669

HARBOROUGH

Factory

B669

Sports Ground

Water Tower

Sports Ground

OAK TREE CL

RUTLAND CT

UNLEY ST

FRASER WAY

LORT ST

MARLOW HOUSE

ALEXANDRA ROAD

ADDISON ROAD

PRINCE RUPERT RD

CROMWELL CL

AVENUE

Sch

BRIDGE ROAD

HILLTOP AV

HILLTOP CL

ASH GROVE

LANGDALE

WHITEHILLS

THE RIDINGS

UPPER DANE

PETREL CL

BRAYBROOKE ROAD

DOVEDALE

EYAM CL

BIRCHVALE

MATLOCK CT

CROMFORD CL

ROAD

NELVILLE WAY

CYPRESS CL

MEISSEN AVENUE

WEDGWOOD CL

WOODWELL HILL

UNITY AVENUE

WINDSOR AV

FEDERATION AVENUE

PIONEER

A6

DESBOROUGH & ROTHWELL BY-

HARRINGTON ROAD

GREEN LANE

A B C D

Rothwell Grange Hospital

Glebe Farm

A14 JUNCTION 7

TELFORD WAY INDUSTRIAL ESTATE

FURNACE LANE

HENSON WAY

TELFORD WAY

HENSON

LINNELL WAY

TORBRIDGE CL

RILEY RD

WYNDHAM

ROBINSON WAY

ROBINSON CL

ENTERPRISE

TELFORD WAY

BARTLEY DR

BARON AV

INDUSTRIAL ESTATE

Kettering Crematorium

HENSON

TELFORD

GARRARD WAY

BUSH ACRE CT

GIPSY

CARRINGTON

HAWESWATER RD

LANGSETT CL

BUTTERMERE CL

THIRLMERE CL

ULLSWATER RD

Amb Sta

LEGION CRES

ROTHWELL R D

14

Wor

ST

HOSPITAL

GIPSY LANE

KETTERING

WINDERMERE

CONISTON ROAD

DERWENT CRES

DERWENT CRES

GRASMERE RD

BOWHILL

ENNER

Sch

WESTOVER RD

WESTHILL DR

WESTHILL CL

WEST W

WESTHILL DR

FURLONG

WEST W

Sch

NORTHAMP

GIPSY LANE

B5323

16

GREENHILL AVENUE

GREENHILL RD

GREENHILL RD

HALL LANE

HALL CLOSE

HALL LA

Sch

Sch

A43

MOORHOUSE WY

FOSTER

BIGNAL CL

BACKLEY CL

LAKE

LONSBOROUGH DR

WELLS CL

MEAD RD

DAWES RD

HEMERY

BROOM WY

WILKIE CL

LINGHAM

THOMPSON WY

CHRISTIE WY

TORVILL

AVENUE

BOARDMAN RD

JACKSON

GUNNELL

PACKER ROAD

BRAITHWAITE

GRANT CL

Sch

REDGRAVE CL

MERRI VALE CLOSE

OLYMPIC WAY

THURS

Sp Ce

K

A14 JUNCTION 8

Northfield Farm

Bottom Lodge Farm

NORTHFIELD ROAD

ROAD

A43

GIPSY ROAD

LANE

WOR

E
F
G
H
1
2
3
4
5
6
A43
WEEKLEY WOOD LANE
STAMFORD ROAD
Boughton Park
Star Pond
Wilderness Spinney
Cricket Ground
Weekley
Ash Bed
Osier Bed
Playing Field
PIPE LANE
GLEBE ROAD
Warkton
Hall
Fedwells Farm
River Ise
WARKTON LANE
Camping & Caravan Site
BRIAR RD
PARADE
HEATHER RD
CHASTON PL
GORSE ROAD
MYRTLE RD
CENTRE
BLUEBELL CL
EDITH ROAD
CORA ROAD
DORIS RD
SHEILA PL
HILDA PL
CHARLOTTE PL
BERTHA WY
KATHLEEN DR
LOUISA DR
JUDITH ROAD
DOROTHY ROAD
JEAN ROAD
RUTH GDNS
MARGARET ROAD
ELIZABETH ROAD
Sch
LIME RD
MAPLE
NASEBY ROAD
EDGAR RD
ALTHORPE PL
LYVEDEN PL
CENTRAL AV
WALK
ATHELSTAN
CARDIGAN PL
NASEBY
COMPTON PL
GLAISTER PL
VALLEY WK
AVENUE
EAST CL
EAST DR
SOUTHGATE DRIVE
Playing Field
DEEBLE ROAD
ST SWITHINS
ST AMANDAS CL
ST NICHOLAS CL
ST VINCENTS
ST MAGDALENES RD
AVENUE
ST VALENTINES CL
SAINT
ST DAVIDS CL
CATHERINES ROAD
ST BARTHOLOMEWS CL
ST BARNABAS CL
ST JOSEPHS CL
ST PHILIPS CL
ALANBROOKE CL
WAVELL CL
ANDERSON
17
Sch

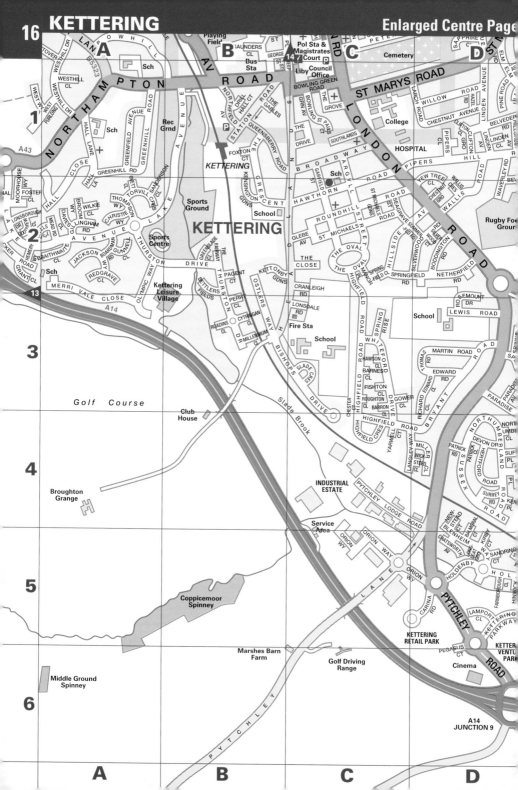

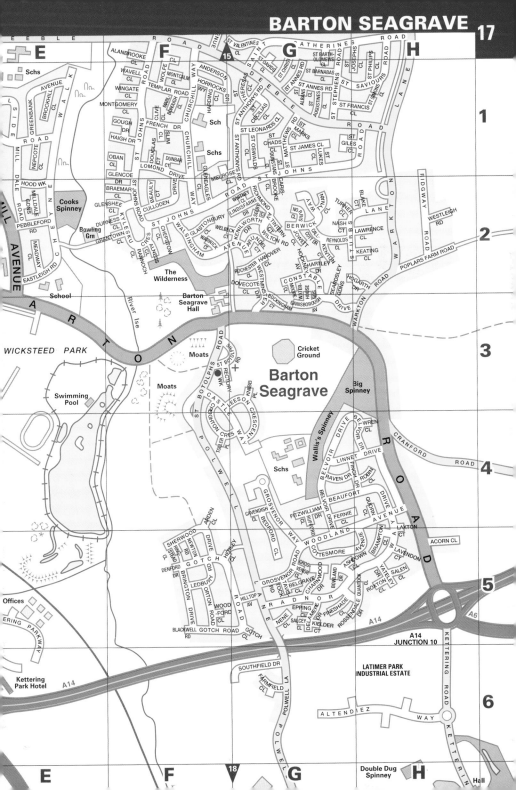

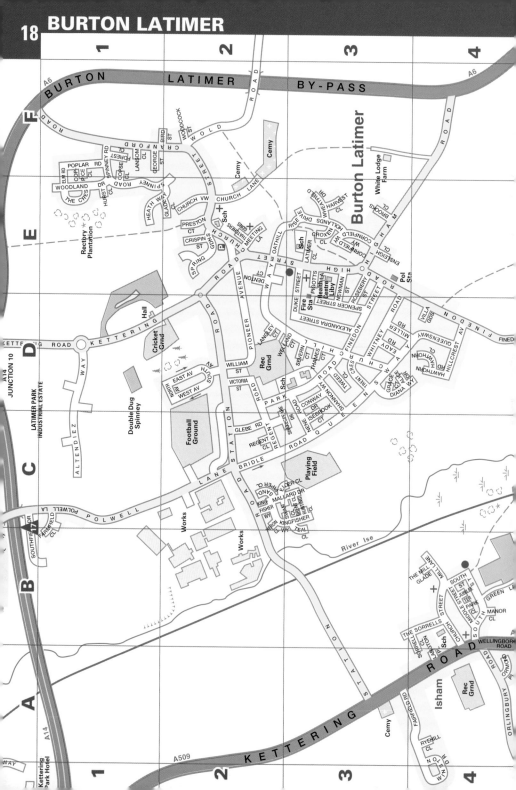

Burton Latimer

BURTON LATIMER BY-PASS

A6

A14 JUNCTION 10

LATIMER PARK INDUSTRIAL ESTATE

Rectory Plantation

Double Dug Spinney

Football Ground

Cricket Grnd

Rec Grnd

Playing Field

River Ise

Works

Isham ROAD

KETTERING ROAD

A509

Kettering Park Hotel

White Lodge Farm

Wellingborough Road

Cemy

Rec Grnd

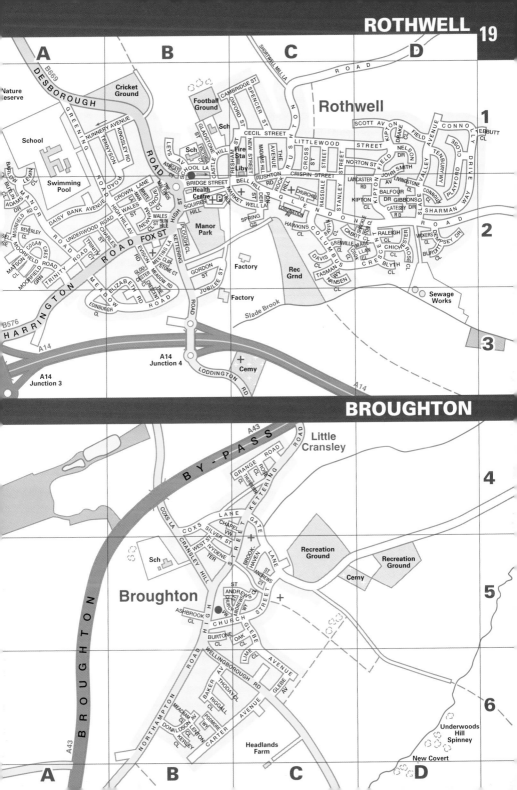

A B C D

1

Top
Lodge

Medieval Village
of Mallows Cotton
(site of)

2

River Nene Navigation

Hog Dyke

M E A D O W

3

Nene Way

Sewage
Works

4

CASTERTON CL
ADAMS CL
COLLINGHAM CL
COURTMAN RD
MANNINGHAM RD
CLEBURNE CL
LOVELL CT
KETENHALL RD
POTTER CT
CUMBERLAND AV
RO

5

NEEDHAM ROAD
ST ALFRED ST
ST LAURENCE WY
RECTORY CL
MANSFIELD ST
Club
JOHN EAGLE CL
DOLBEN AVENUE
GREEN LA
PARKLY
SONLY
R A U N D S
Primary
School

Sand &
Gravel Pit

Sewage
Works

Stanwick

Nursing
Home

Hall

MANOR GDNS
CHURCH
COURTWOOD
NEWBRIDGE ST
CHAPEL LA
THE AVENUE
BROOKSIDE ST

VILLA LANE
SAMUELS LA
HIGH STREET
SPENCER PARADE
STREET
WEST
GRANGE
HILL HOUSE GDNS

6

River Nene

The Hall

PRIMROSE CL
HIGHAM RD

ROAD EAST

The Hay
Barn

Hall
Farm

MARKS
CL
Orchard
Farm

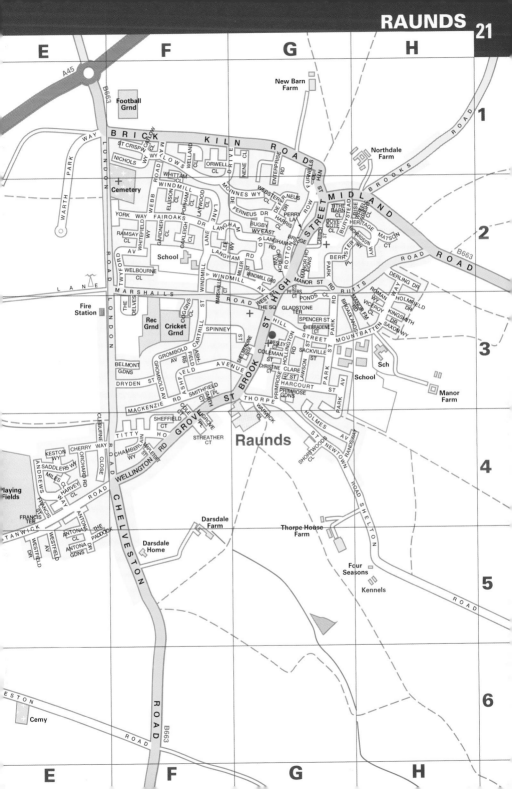

E   F   G   H

A45
B663

New Barn Farm

Football Grnd

1

BRICK KILN ROAD
ST CRISPIN WY
NICHOLS
WHITTAM CL
WINDMILL
WEBB
YORK WAY
FAIROAKS
RAMSAY CL
WHITEFIELD
GARDNER CL
OAKLEIGH CL
School
WELBOURNE CL

Cemetery

MALLOWS WY
ORWELL CL
NENE CL
ENTERPRISE RD
McINNES WY
PORHAM CL
LAYWOOD DR
LANGHAM LANE
LEE WY
LANGHAM RD
FERNEUS DR
RUGBY WY EAST
LANGHAM RD
MILLER RD
WINDMILL GRO
WINDMILL AV

OLIVE
WEBSTER CL
NEUS
JETER DR
HARRIS CL
BRIDGE ST
ROTTON ROW
MANOR RD GDNS
MANOR RD
PETERS
PONDS CL
GLADSTONE TER
SPENCER ST
CHEBRADENE CT

Northdale Farm

MIDLAND ROAD

B663 ROAD

CORNELLS
LITTLE BARN CL
BURY STEAD
DOVECOTE
BERRYSTEAD
BERT PL
RISE
HERITAGE
RICHARDSON WY
MATSON CT

2

DERLING DR
ROMAN WAY
HOLMFIELD
VICEROY
KINGSMITH DR
SAXON WY
BUTTS
BROADLANDS

LANE
LONDON ROAD
MARSHAILS
THE DELVES
Fire Station
Rec Grnd
Cricket Grnd
COGGINS AV
SPINNEY
CARTRILL
GROMBOLD AV
BELMONT GDNS
DRYDEN ST
ASHFIELD RD
SMITHFIELD
MACKENZIE RD
SHEFFIELD

WEST ST
THE SQ
HILL STREET
WESLEYGTON RD
COLEMAN ST
CHRISTINE CL
JOSEPHINE
PRIMROSE
SACKVILLE ST
CLARE ST
HARCOURT ST
PRIMROSE GDNS
THORPE ST
WARWICK

BROADENE CT
PARK RD
MOUNTBATTEN
PARK ST
PARK AV
LAWSON ST

3

Sch
School
Manor Farm

CLEBURNE WAY
CHERRY WAY
KESTON WY
SADDLERS WY
ORCHARD RD
ANDREWS
MILES CL
HARVEY CL
FRANCIS WAY
GROVE
MAPLESIDE
CHAMBERLAIN WY
TITTY HO
SHEFFIELD
KILBROOKE CT
STREATHER CT

Raunds

HOLMES AV
RANDSMAN
SHORTWOOD CL
NEWTOWN

4

Playing Fields
FRANCIS TER
ANTONA CL
ANTONA GDNS
WESTFIELD DR
WESTFIELD AV
THE PADDOCK
STANWICK

WELLINGTON RD
CHELVESTON ROAD

Darsdale Farm
Darsdale Home

Thorpe House Farm

SHELTON

Four Seasons
Kennels

5

ROAD

ESTON
Cemy

ROAD
B663

6

E   F   G   H

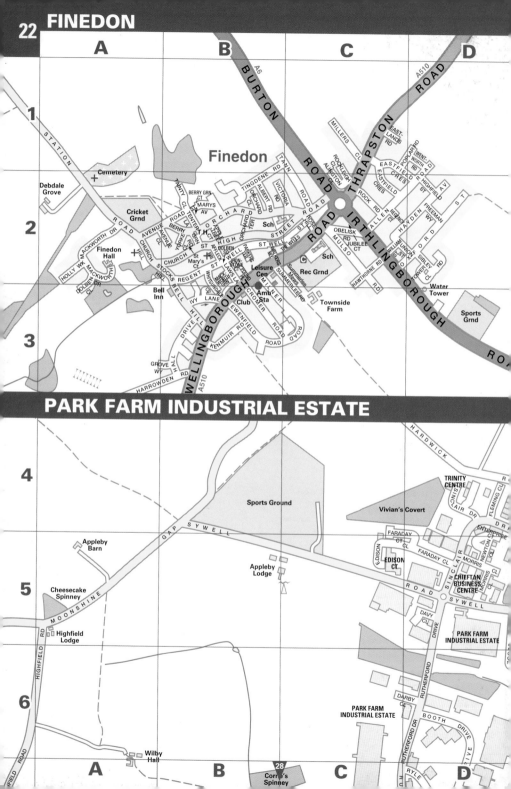

A B C D

1

Finedon

STATION ROAD

A6 BURTON ROAD

A510 ROAD

MILLERS
EAST-LANDS RD
WENT- CL
APWORTH CL
WORTH RD
G HIGHFIELD

Debdale
Grove

Cemetery

EASTFIELD CRES
EASTFIELD RD
EASTFIELD CRES

2

Cricket
Grnd

Finedon
Hall

HOLLY WK MACKWORTH DR
MACKWORTH
DOLBEN DR
CL

AVENUE
BERRY
AVE
YORKE ST
CHURCH HILL
STOCKS HILL
HILL
REGENT

BERRY GRN CT
MARYS AV
ST MARYS
ORCHARD RD
ORCHARD CL
ALBERT RD
VICTORIA
TANN RD
TINGDENE RD

ORCHARD
T.H.
St Mary's
DOLBEN
ST WELL
IRON
STONE
LAWSLEY
WHITWORTH
MACKIE
CROMER
IVY LANE
EWENFIELD

HIGH
ST
DOLBEN ST
PANTER
WELL ST
SUMMERLEA RD
ST WELL
THE WELLS ST
Summerlea
MEWS

STREET
VICTORIA ST
ROAD

Sch

Leisure
Cen

Bell
Inn

Club

Amb'
Sta

MILNER

DRIVE
A510 WELLINGBOROUGH
HILL
GROVE WY
HARROWDEN HALL
KENMUIR
WELLINGBOROUGH ROAD
CROMER ROAD
ROSE ROAD

3

THRAPSTON ROAD
IRTHLINGBOROUGH ROAD

ROCKLEIGH RD
CLICKTON
ALINGTON
ROCK RD
ALLEN RD

OBELISK RD
JUBILEE CT
MULSO
C
Rec Grnd

Sch

HAWTHORNE RD

POPLAR
NORTH A
ASH RD
G HIGHFIELD

REGINALD ST
FREEMAN WY
HAYDEN RD
WILLIAM UNION
SIBLEY
CL

Water
Tower

Townside
Farm

Sports
Grnd

ROAD

4

HARDWICK

Sports Ground

Vivian's Covert

TRINITY
CENTRE
R
SINCLAIR DR
FLEMING CL
ENTERPRISE

GAP SYWELL

FARADAY CT CL
EDISON
FARADAY CL
MORRIS
NEWTON CL
MORRIS CL

Appleby
Barn

Appleby
Lodge

EDISON
CT

CHIEFTAN
BUSINESS
CENTRE

5

Cheesecake
Spinney

MOONSHINE

ROAD

SYWELL

Highfield
Lodge

RD

DAVY
CL

DRIVE

PARK FARM
INDUSTRIAL ESTATE

HIGHFIELD RD

RUTHERFORD

6

DARBY
CL

PARK FARM
INDUSTRIAL ESTATE

BOOTH DRIVE

RUTHERFORD DR

RYLE

Wilby
Hall

28
Corre's
Spinney

A B C D

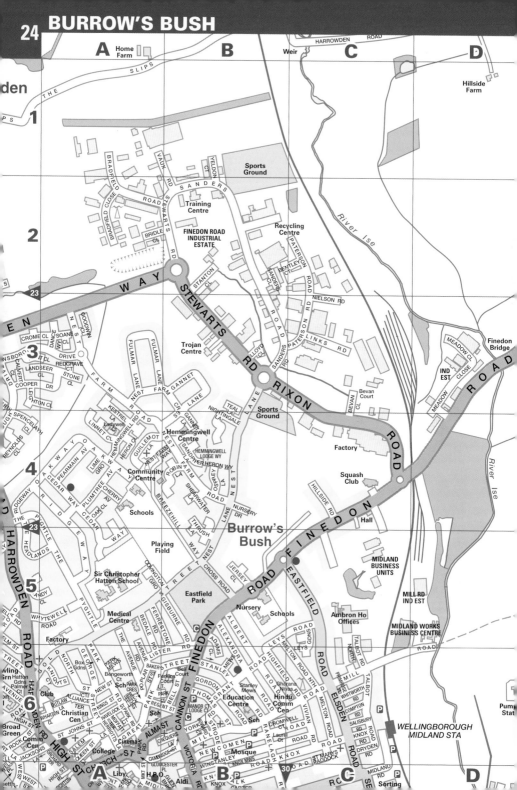

Burrow's Bush

WELLINGBOROUGH MIDLAND STA

E   F   G   H

Nevilles Lodge

RYEBURY HILL

Ryebury Farm

Quarry

Sidegate Landfill

egate orks

SIDEGATE

Factory

Carrol Spring Farm

Refuse Tip

Top Lodge Farm

West Field Lodge

rks

Finedonhill Farm

Stone Cross Farm

WELLIN

B571

WELLINGBOROUGH RD

LANE

ROAD

DITCHFORD

South Hill Farm

South View Farm

Waverly Cottages

IRTHLINGBOROUGH

ROAD

DITCHFORD RD

Kennels

Grange Farm

Irthlingborough Grange

Works

Weir

Sand and Gravel Pit

B571

E   F   G   H   DITCH

INGBOROUGH ROAD

1

2

26

3

4

26

5

6

31

A B C D

1
2
3
4
5
6

Huxlow School 36

Central Recreation Ground

Sports Ground

Cricket Ground

Factory

NURSERY GDNS
Schs
Civic Hall
Market Cross
Work
Liby
STATION

SCARBOROUGH ST
MANTON CL
EXCELSIOR RD
MUSSON CL
Surgery
Louisa Lilley Homes
Cemy

JUBILEE ST
QUEEN ST
Hargrave St
Works
Liby
Med Cen
Irthlingborou

WINDMILL RD
Club
Amb Sta
Hall
Pol Ho
GEORGE ST
VICTORIA RD
SPENCER RD
WHITES RD
CHERRY ST
NICHOLS RD

B571
Nursing Home
ALLEN
COWPER RD
BRIGHTWELL
FLAWN
DIAMOND CT
PERKINS
EXPRESS
VALE
WAY

TANNERY COTTS

WELLINGBOROUGH ROAD

West Field Lodge

Cemetery
Chapel

THE WK
EVENSFORD
SIDINGS
WATERLOO WAY
LAKESIDE
CRESS WK
WEBB
DAIRY WK
HOME CL
LODGE WAY

B571 WELLINGBOROUGH RD

Broadholme

Sewage Works

River Nene

25
25

River Nene
Weir

Weir
Works

Skew Bridge Ski Lake

Nene Valley Farm
Club
Bowling Green

ROAD
DITCHFORD
A45
RTHAMPTON

A B C D

32

A   **B**   22   **C**   **D**

HIGHFIELD RD

Wilby Hall

Corrie's Spinney

PARK FARM INDUSTRIAL ESTATE

RUTHERFO

RYLE

HUXLEY

HUXLEY CL

CLOSE

RUTHERFORD

DRIVE

BOOTH

DENCORA BUSINESS PARK

NAPIER CL

WALLIS CL

DRIVE

1

The Rookery

The Grange

The Golsa

P A R K

2

Cromwell Spinney

Alla Barn

3

W I L B Y   R O A D

W I L B Y

Wilby Spinney

Glebe Barn

Glebe Farm

R O A D

4

Th

5

M A I N

R O A D

6

Field Barn

Hockerhill Farm

Brookhill Farm

Wilby Bridge

R O A D   M A I N

A4500

A   **B**   34   **C**   **D**

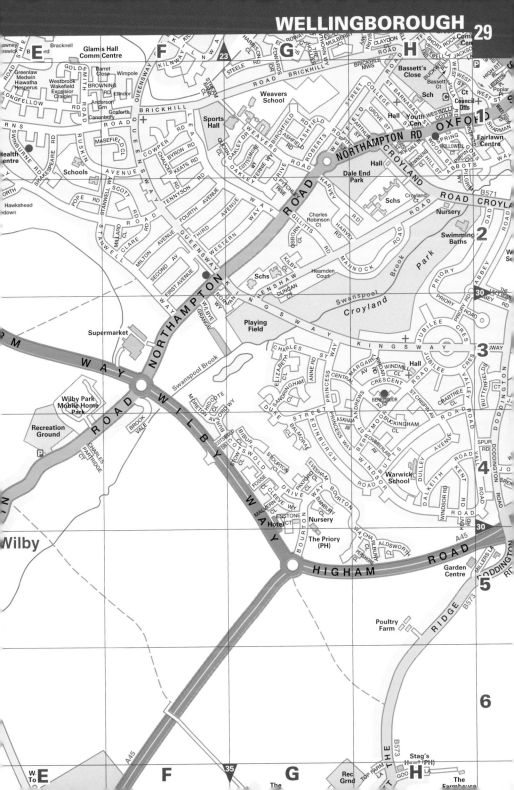

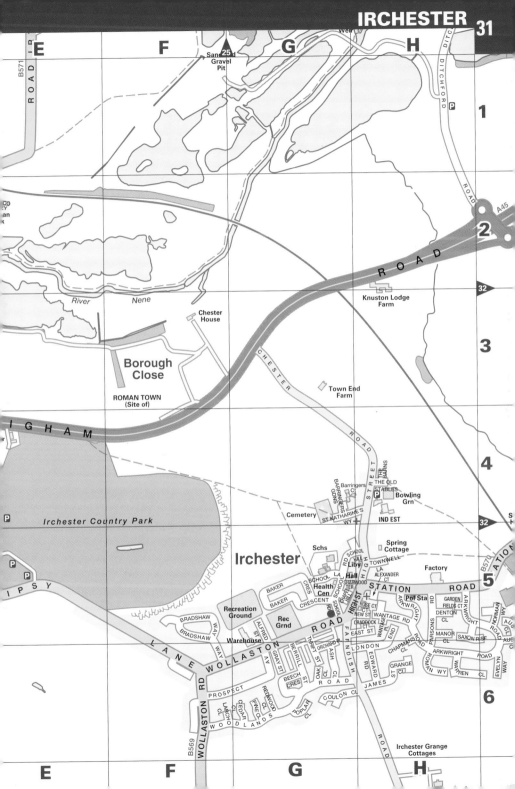

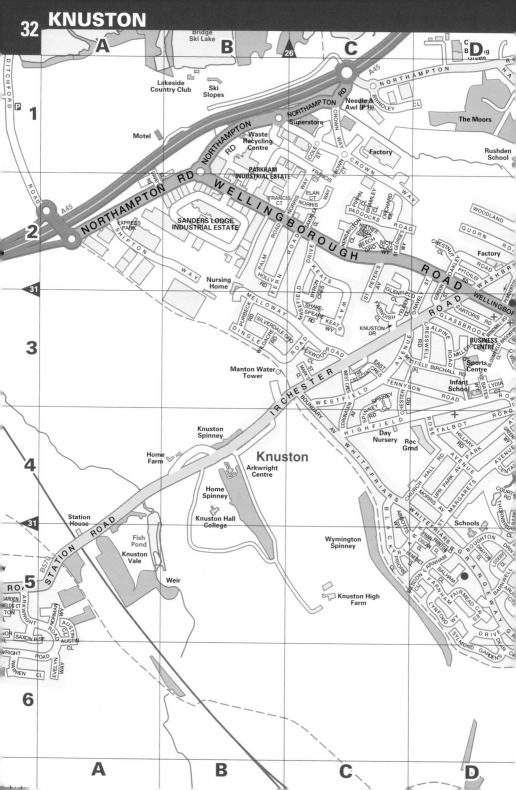

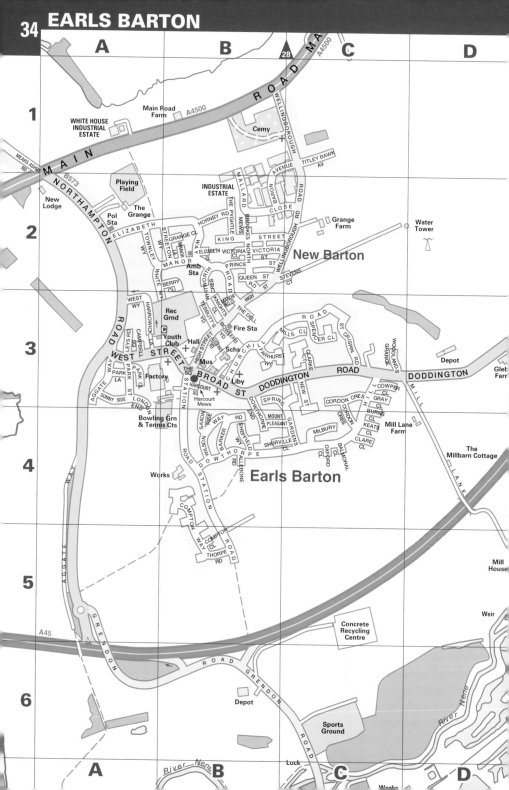

A   **B**   28   **C**   **D**

MAIN ROAD MA

A4500

MEARS ASHBY RD

MAIN

NORTHAMPTON

B573

Main Road Farm   A4500

WHITE HOUSE INDUSTRIAL ESTATE

WELLINGBOROUGH ROAD

Cemy

TITLEY BAWK AV

AVENUE

MALLARD

BROOKES CLOSE

New Lodge

Playing Field

Pol Sta

The Grange

ELIZABETH

TOWNLEY WY

STREETON

GRANGE CL

MANOR

THE PYGHTLE

MEWS

HORNBY RD

ELIZABETH CL

KING STREET

Grange Farm

Water Tower

WHITE

BERRY CL

WEST WY

HARROWICK

MANOR

AMB Sta

PRINCE

VICTORIA CL

QUEEN ST

VICTORIA ST

ST

STEVENS CT

WELLINGBOROUGH RD

NORTH

New Barton

Rec Grnd

Youth Club

WILLIAM STREET

JEBB'S

KNIGHTS RD

TEBBUTT'S YD

BOWLERS

CLOSE

Fire Sta

THE DELL

HIGH

MANOR RD

ROAD

SPENCER CL

ST CRISPIN RD

WOODLANDS

GRANGE

Depot

ROAD

Hall

Schs

CHURCHILL

FAIRHURST WY

MILLS CL

CLARKE CT

WEST STREET

CAMPBELL SQ

B573

Mus

THE SQ

Liby

BROAD ST

STATION

DODDINGTON

ROAD

DODDINGTON

MILL LANE

Gleb Farr

PARK LA

SUNNY SIDE

PARK ST

LONG ENDE

Factory

Harcourt SQ

Harcourt Mews

SPRING

DOWTHORPE END

NEW ST

CORDON CRES

COWPER CL

GRAY CL

BURNS CL

KEATS CL

CLARE CL

Mill Lane Farm

BALMORAL

OXFORD

AGGATE WAY

Bowling Grn & Tennis Cts

SAXON WAY

BARKER RD

SHEFFIELD WY

ALLEBONE

MOUNT PLEASANT

SHURVILLE CL

GARDENS

MILBURY

CORDON CRES

CLARE CL

Earls Barton

The Millbarn Cottage

Works

ROAD

STATION

DOWTHORPE

THORPE

LANE

COMPTON WAY

COMPTON WY CL

THORPE RD

ROAD

Mill House

Weir

AGGATE

GRENDON

A45

Concrete Recycling Centre

River Nene

ROAD

GRENDON

Depot

GRENDON ROAD

Sports Ground

River Nene

River Nene

Lock

Works

A   **B**   **C**   **D**

1   2   3   4   5   6

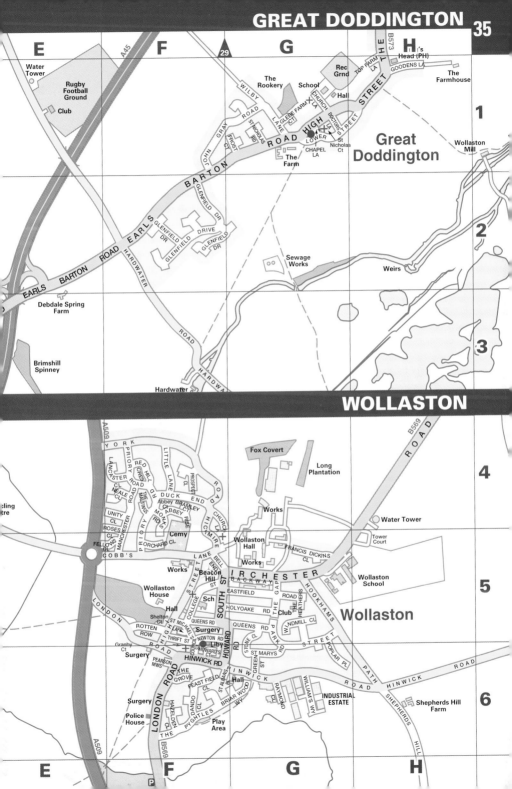

E   A45   **F**   29   **G**   B573   THE   **H** 's Head (PH)

Water Tower

Rugby Football Ground

Club

The Rookery

School

Rec Grnd

Top Farm

Hall

GOODENS LA

The Farmhouse

1

WILBY LANE

GRAY CT

JOHN

FROST CT

ST NICHOLAS RD

BARTON

ROAD

HIGH

GLEBE FARM CT

DODDING STREET

CHURCH STREET

LOWER

CHAPEL LA

St Nicholas Ct

STREET

The Farm

Great Doddington

Wollaston Mill

EARLS

HARDWATER

GLENFIELD DR

GLENFIELD DRIVE

GLENFIELD DR

GLENFIELD DR

Sewage Works

Weirs

2

EARLS BARTON ROAD

Debdale Spring Farm

Brimshill Spinney

ROAD

HARDWA

HARDWATER

Hardwater

3

A509

YORK

PRIORY ROAD

LANCASTER

NEALE CL

UNITY CL

ROSES CL

FELLOWS CL

LITTLE LANE

RED HILL

CRESS RD

TWELVETREE

MANCHESTER

COBB'S

Abbey CL

MO ABBEY RD

BRAWLEY RISE

PRIORY DR

ORCHARD CL

Cemy

ROAD

PROSPECT CL

LANE END

DUCK

HICKMIRE

CHURCH

LANE

Fox Covert

Works

Long Plantation

B569

ROAD

Water Tower

Tower Court

4

eling tre

LONDON

BELL STREET

COLLEGE STREET

ST MICHAELS CL

SOUTH

Works

Beacon Hill ST

Sch

EASTFIELD

HOLYOAKE RD

Wollaston Hall

FRANCIS DICKINS

IRCHESTER

BACKWAY

THE GAP

ROAD

Club

WNDMILL CL

HOOKHAMS

THE HEATHERS

Wollaston School

Wollaston

5

Wollaston House

Hall

Shelton CL

ROTTEN ROW

Granby Ct

Surgery

ROAD

Thrift St

HAYARDS

NEWTON RD

Surgery

HINWICK RD

QUEENS RD

QUEENS RD

STONE CL

ST MARYS

PARK

POPLAR PL

STREET

Wollaston

PEARSON MWS

FEAST FIELD CL

ST ALBANS

INWICK

GREEN END

WILLIAMS WY

RAYMOND

HINWICK

ROAD

ROAD

Surgery

Police House

THE GROVE

HAZELDEN

THE PYGHTLES

DANDO CL

BRIAR WOOD WY

Play Area

Hall

INDUSTRIAL ESTATE

SHEPHERDS

HILL

Shepherds Hill Farm

6

A509

B569

E   **F**   **G**   **H**

Irthlingborough

A - Z INDEX TO STREETS
with Postcodes

The Index includes some names for which there is insufficient space on the maps. These names are indicated by an * and are followed by the nearest adjoining thoroughfare.

Abbey Ct NN29 35 F4
Abbey Rd NN8 30 A2
Abbey Rise NN29 35 F4
Abbey St LE16 5 C5
Abbey Way NN10 33 E5
Abbots Way NN8 29 H1
Abbotts Way NN10 32 C4
Abington Rd NN17 6 B5
Acorn Cl NN15 17 H5
Acre St NN16 14 D5
Adam & Eve St LE16 5 C5
Adams Cl, Stanwick NN9 20 D4
Adams Cl, Wellingborough NN8 24 B5
Adams Dr NN14 19 A2
Adamswood Cl LE16 5 A5
Addington Rd NN9 36 B4
Addison Rd NN14 12 B3
Adit Vw NN9 26 B3
Adnitt Rd NN10 32 D3
Afan Cl NN16 14 B2
Affleck Bri NN9 22 B2
Aggate Way NN6 34 A3
Aggate Way NN6 34 A5
Aintree Dr NN10 33 G5
Alanbrooke Cl NN15 15 F6
Albany Gdns NN18 8 C4
Albert Rd, Finedon NN9 22 B2
Albert Rd, Market Harborough LE16 5 D5
Albert Rd, Rushden NN10 33 F3
Albert Rd, Wellingborough NN8 24 B5
Albert St NN16 3 D4
Alberta Cl NN18 8 C3
Albion Pl NN10 33 F4
Albion Rd NN16 14 B4
Albisdene Ct NN10 33 G2
Alder Cl NN14 12 F3
Aldsworth Cl NN8 29 H5
Alexander Ct NN29 31 H5
Alexander Pl NN9 36 C2
Alexander Rd NN9 36 C1
Alexandra Rd, Corby NN17 3 A2
Alexandra Rd, Kettering NN14 12 B2
Alexandra Rd, Rushden NN10 33 H3
Alexandra Rd, Wellingborough NN8 24 B5
Alexandra St, Burton Latimer NN15 18 D3
Alexandra St, Kettering NN16 3 C4
Alfoxden NN8 29 E2
Alfred St, Irchester NN29 31 G5
Alfred St, Kettering NN16 3 C4
Alfred St, Rushden NN10 33 E3
Alfred St, Stanwick NN9 20 C5
Alice Dr NN15 18 D3
Alice Gdns*, Judith Rd NN16 15 E4
Alington Cl NN9 22 C1
Allebone Rd NN6 34 B4
Allen Rd, Finedon NN9 22 C2
Allen Rd, Irthlingborough NN9 36 A5
Allen Rd, Rushden NN10 33 F2
Alliance Ct NN8 24 A6
Alliance Ter NN8 24 A6
Alma St NN8 24 A6
Almond Rd NN16 14 D4
Alness Cl NN15 17 F2
Alpine Rd NN10 32 D3
Altendiez Way NN15 17 G6
Althorp Cl, Market Harborough LE16 5 F6
Althorp Cl, Wellingborough NN8 23 F4
Althorp Pl NN18 8 C3
Althorpe Pl NN16 15 E5
Alvington Way LE16 4 B4
Ambleside Cl NN8 23 F6
Anderson Dr NN15 17 F1
Anderson Grn NN8 29 E1
Andrew Cl NN10 27 F4
Andrew MacDonald Cl LE16 5 D5
Andrews Way NN9 21 E4
Angel Ct LE16 5 C5
Angel La NN8 30 A1
Annandale Rd NN17 6 D5
Anne Cl NN10 27 F4
Anne Rd NN8 29 G3
Anne Sq*, Jean Rd NN16 15 E4
Anne St NN17 3 A2
Anne Walk*, Beech Cl NN17 6 D3
Anson Cl NN17 6 B5
Antona Cl NN9 21 E5
Antona Dr NN9 21 E4
Antona Gdns NN9 21 E5
Appleby Cl NN9 23 H2
Applegarth Cl NN18 9 E4
Appletree Ct NN9 22 B2
Archfield NN8 29 H1
Archfield Ter NN9 36 B3
Arden Cl, Kettering NN15 17 F4
Arden Cl, Market Harborough LE16 4 E4
Arden Way LE16 4 D4
Argyle Pk LE16 5 C8
Argyll St, Corby NN17 3 B2
Argyll St, Kettering NN15 16 C1
Arkwright Rd, Corby NN17 7 H3
Arkwright Rd, Wellingborough NN29 31 H5
Arnsley Rd NN17 10 D2
Arran Way NN17 6 B4
Arthingworth Rd NN14 12 A2
Arthur St NN8 29 H1
Arthurs Walk*, Alexandra St NN16 3 D4
Arum Cl NN10 33 F6
Arundel Ct, Kettering NN15 17 G2
Arundel Ct, Rushden NN10 32 D5
Arundel Walk NN18 8 C1
Ascot Rd NN10 33 G5
Ash Cl NN29 31 G6
Ash Gro NN14 12 A2
Ash Rd NN15 16 D1
Ashbourne Dr NN14 12 A2
Ashbrook Cl NN14 19 B5
Ashby Cl NN8 23 G3
Ashby Dr NN10 33 E5
Ashdown Cl NN15 17 G5
Ashdown Pl NN17 7 E5
Ashfield Av NN9 21 F3
Ashfield Rd, Market Harborough LE16 5 C5
Ashfield Rd, Wellingborough NN8 29 G1
Ashfield Rise NN9 21 F3
Ashford Lea NN14 12 A2
Ashgate Ct NN14 19 B1
Ashleigh Ho*, Rectory Ct NN10 33 E3
Ashley Av NN17 6 B5
Ashley Ct NN16 14 B5
Ashley Rd NN16 11 B1
Ashley Ter LE16 5 F5
Ashley Way LE16 5 F5
Ashridge Cl NN10 32 D5
Ashton Gro NN8 23 F3
Ashurst Cres NN18 8 C1
Ashwell Rd NN10 33 G3
Askham Av NN8 29 G4
Aspen Cl NN10 33 E2
Aster Rd NN16 14 D3
Astley Cl LE16 5 B7
Athelstan Rd NN16 15 E5
Attley Ct NN8 23 F6
Attley Way NN9 36 C3
Auden Way NN17 6 B4
Audley Cl LE16 5 F6
Auriga St LE16 5 D6
Austin Cl NN29 32 A5
Austin Ho*, High St NN14 19 B2
Austins Cl LE16 5 B5
Austins Yd NN6 34 B3
Avalon Ct*, Cross St NN14 19 C1
Avenue Cl NN9 22 A2
Avenue Rd, Finedon NN9 22 A2
Avenue Rd, Wellingborough NN8 24 A5
Avon Cl, Kettering NN16 14 B3
Avon Cl, Wellingborough NN8 23 F4
Avondale Rd NN16 14 D4
Aynsley Cl NN14 12 B3

Backley Cl NN15 13 C6
Backway NN29 35 G5
Baffin Cl NN14 19 C2
Bailey Ct NN10 27 E6
Baird Ct NN8 23 E5
Baird Rd NN17 10 A1
Bakehouse La*, Kettering Rd NN15 18 E2
Baker Av NN14 19 B6
Baker Cres NN29 31 G5
Baker St, Irthlingborough NN9 36 A5
Baker St, Wellingborough NN8 24 A6
Balcombe Pl NN18 8 B1
Balfour Dr NN14 19 D2
Balfour Gdns LE16 5 B7
Balfour St NN16 14 C3
Balham Cl NN10 32 D5
Ballantyne Rd NN10 32 D4
Balmoral NN18 8 D3
Balmoral Av NN10 33 F2
Balmoral Cl, Market Harborough LE16 5 F6
Balmoral Cl, Northampton NN6 34 C4
Balmoral Cl, Wellingborough NN8 29 G4
Balmoral Ct NN15 16 D5
Baltic Cl NN18 8 B4
Bamburg Cl NN18 8 B5
Bamburgh Cl LE16 5 F5
Bampton Ct NN18 9 F2
Banbury Cl NN8 29 G4
Bancroft Rd NN16 11 D1
Bangrave Rd NN17 10 C4
Bankfield Dr LE16 4 E3
Bankside NN18 9 E3
Banner Cl NN10 32 D4
Bardsley Rd NN17 6 D1
Barker Cl NN10 33 F3
Barker Rd NN6 34 B4
Barlow Cl NN14 19 A1
Barn Cl NN18 8 C5
Barnard NN18 8 D3
Barnard Gdns LE16 5 B8
Barnes Cl NN15 16 C3
Barnwell Dr NN10 32 D5
Barnwell Gdns NN8 23 G3
Barnwell Rd NN8 23 F4
Barnwell St NN16 14 D5
Baron Av, Kettering NN16 13 C2
Baron Av, Northampton NN6 34 B2
Baron Ct NN17 10 C1
Barret Cl NN8 29 E1
Barrett Cl NN10 27 F6
Barringers Ct NN29 31 G4
Barringers Gdns NN29 31 G4
Barrington Rd NN10 33 F5
Barron Cl NN15 16 C3
Barth Cl NN18 8 C4
Bartley Dr NN16 13 D2
Barton Rd NN15 17 E3
Barton Sq NN18 6 B6
Bassett's Cl NN8 29 H1
Bassett's Ct NN8 29 H1
Bates Cl, Market Harborough LE16 4 C3
Bates Cl, Rushden NN10 27 E6
Bath La NN16 14 D5
Bath Rd NN16 14 D5
Bath St LE16 5 C7
Bayes St NN16 14 B5
Baysdale Av NN17 6 D5
Beaconsfield Pl NN10 33 E2
Beaconsfield Ter NN10 33 E2
Beanfield Av NN18 6 B6
Beardsley Ct NN18 9 E1
Beardsley Gdns NN15 17 G2
Beatrice Rd NN16 14 C3
Beatty Gdns NN17 6 A5
Beaufort Dr NN15 17 G4
Beauly Ct NN15 17 F2
Beaumaris Cl NN10 33 G4
Beaumont Cl NN16 14 C1
Beck Ct NN8 23 F5
Bedale Rd NN8 24 A5
Bede Cl, Corby NN18 8 B5
Bede Cl, Rushden NN10 27 F5
Bedford Cl NN15 17 G4
Bedford Rd NN10 33 F5
Beech Cl, Corby NN17 6 D3
Beech Cl, Kettering NN14 12 C3
Beech Cres, Kettering NN15 14 D6
Beech Cres, Wellingborough NN29 31 G6
Beech Dr NN8 23 G6
Beech Gro NN10 32 C2
Beech Rd NN10 33 E1
Beechwood Suite NN8 30 C2
Beeston Pl NN18 8 D1
Belgrave Cl NN15 17 G5
Bell Ct, Corby NN18 9 E2
Bell Ct, Wellingborough NN8 24 B6
Bell End NN29 35 F5
Bell Hill, Kettering NN14 19 C2
Bell Hill, Wellingborough NN9 22 B3
Bell St NN8 24 B6
Bellfields La LE16 5 E6
Bellfields St LE16 5 E6
Belmont Gdns NN9 21 F3
Belvedere Rd NN15 16 D1
Belvoir Cl NN10 33 G5
Belvoir Dr NN15 17 G4
Benedict Cl NN10 32 C5
Bengeworth Ct NN8 24 A6
Benteman Cl NN10 27 E6
Bentley Ct NN8 24 B2
Bentley Walk NN18 8 D2
Berrill St NN29 31 G6
Berrister Pl NN9 21 G2
Berry Cl, Market Harborough LE16 4 E3
Berry Cl, Northampton NN6 34 B2
Berry Field Rd NN16 11 C1
Berry Green Ct NN9 22 B2
Berry Green Rd NN9 22 B2
Berry Green Ter*, Berry Green Rd NN9 22 B2
Berry Rd NN16 11 C1
Berrymoor Ct NN8 29 H3
Berrymoor Rd NN8 29 H4
Bertha Way NN16 15 E4
Berwick Rd NN14 11 B5
Berwick Way NN15 17 G2
Bessemer Gro NN17 7 G6
Bestwood Grn NN18 8 D1
Betony Walk NN10 33 F5
Bevan Cl NN8 24 C3
Bevan Ct NN8 24 C3
Beverley Cl NN14 19 A2
Beverley Rd NN15 16 D2
Beverley Walk*, Thirsk Rd NN18 8 D1
Bewick Ct NN18 9 E1
Bexhill Walk*, Brighton Rd NN18 8 C2
Bibury Cl NN8 29 G4
Bideford Sq NN18 9 G1
Bies Cl NN18 8 D4
Bignal Cl NN15 13 C5
Bilsdon Cl NN10 32 D5
Bilton Ct NN8 23 F6
Binders Ct NN14 11 C5
Bingham Walk NN18 8 D1
Birch Av NN18 9 E2
Birch Rd, Kettering NN16 15 E4
Birch Rd, Rushden NN10 33 G3
Birch Tree Gdns LE16 4 D4
Birchall Rd NN10 32 D3
Birchfield Rd NN8 29 G1
Birchington Rd NN17 10 C1
Birchvale Ct NN14 12 A2
Bird St NN15 18 F2
Birkdale Dr NN10 33 G4
Birling Pl NN18 8 B1
Birtley Coppice LE16 4 B4
Bishop Cl LE16 5 C8
Bishops Ct NN10 27 F4
Bishops Dr NN15 16 B3
Blackberry Cl NN16 14 C1
Blackfriars NN10 32 C4
Blackmoor Av NN18 9 F2
Blackthorn Cl NN16 14 C2
Blackwell Rd NN15 17 F5
Blake Ct NN15 17 H2
Blake Rd NN18 9 E1
Blake Walk NN10 27 E6
Blandford Ct NN18 6 A6
Blanford Av NN16 14 B3
Blaydon Walk NN8 23 G4
Bleaklow Cl NN14 12 A2
Blenheim Cl NN10 33 E5
Blenheim Rd NN8 23 G4
Blenheim Walk NN18 8 D3
Blenheim Way, Kettering NN15 16 D4
Blenheim Way, Market Harborough LE16 4 C4
Blinco Rd NN10 33 F3
Blind La NN16 11 D1
Bloomfield Cl NN10 32 D3
Bluebell Cl, Corby NN18 9 E4
Bluebell Cl, Kettering NN16 15 E4
Bluebell Rise NN10 33 F5
Blyth Cl NN14 19 D2
Blyton Cl NN18 8 D2
Board St NN9 36 B4
Boardman Rd NN15 16 A2
Boddington Rd NN15 16 D2
Boden Cl NN18 8 B4
Bodiam Pl NN18 8 B1
Bognor Rd NN18 8 B2
Bonham Ct NN16 14 D5
Bonnington Walk NN18 9 E1
Booth Dr NN8 22 D6
Borough Ct*, Westfields Av NN10 27 F6
Borrowdale Rd NN17 6 D4
Boston Cl NN18 8 C2
Boughton Cl NN18 8 B2
Boughton Dr NN10 32 D5
Boundary Av NN10 32 C3
Bourne Cl NN8 23 E5
Bourton Way NN8 29 G5
Bowden La LE16 5 C5
Bowden Ridge LE16 4 E4
Bowhill NN16 14 A6
Bowland Dr NN15 17 G5
Bowlers Yd NN6 34 B3
Bowling Green Av NN15 3 B6
Bowling Green Rd NN15 3 B6
Bowness NN8 23 F6
Box Gdns NN8 24 A6
Boyle Rd NN17 10 A2
Bracadale Way*, Shire Rd NN17 6 C3
Bracken Cl NN16 14 B2
Bradfield Cl, Rushden NN10 33 G2
Bradfield Cl, Wellingborough NN8 24 A2
Bradfield Rd NN8 24 A1
Bradford Walk*, York Rd NN18 8 C1
Bradmore Gdns NN18 6 C6
Bradshaw Way NN29 31 F5
Braemar Cl NN15 17 F2
Braid Ct NN8 23 F4
Braithwaite Cl NN15 13 D6
Brakey Rd NN17 10 C2
Bramber Ct NN18 8 B1
Bramble Cl NN16 14 C2
Brambleside NN16 14 C2
Brambleside Ct NN16 14 C2
Bramblewood Rd NN17 10 E3
Bramley Cl, Market Harborough LE16 4 D4
Bramley Cl, Rushden NN10 32 C2
Bramley Ct NN29 35 F4
Brampton Cl, Kettering NN15 17 H5
Brampton Cl, Wellingborough NN8 23 G4
Bramshill Av NN16 14 B2
Brandenburg Rd NN18 8 A4
Brangwyn Walk NN18 9 E1
Branksome Ct NN18 6 A6
Braunton Pl NN18 9 G2
Brawn Cl NN9 26 C3
Braybrooke Rd, Kettering NN14 12 A2
Braybrooke Rd, Market Harborough LE16 5 E7
Brayford Av NN18 9 F1
Breakleys Rd NN14 12 D3
Breck Cl NN18 8 C6
Brecon Cl NN16 14 C1
Breedon Cl NN18 8 B5
Breezehill Way NN8 24 A4
Brent Cl NN15 18 C3
Briar Ct NN9 36 B5
Briar Rd NN16 15 E3
Briar Wood Way NN29 35 F6
Brick Kiln Rd NN9 21 F1
Brickhill Mews NN8 29 H1
Brickhill Rd NN8 29 F1
Brideswell La*, Horse Market NN16 3 C4
Bridge Ct NN17 7 G5
Bridge Rd NN14 12 B2
Bridge St, Corby NN17 10 E3
Bridge St, Kettering NN14 19 B2
Bridge St, Wellingborough NN9 21 G2
Bridgford Pl NN18 6 B6
Bridgwater Ct NN18 6 A6
Bridle Cl NN8 24 A2
Bridle Rd NN15 18 C2
Briery Cl NN18 8 C5
Brigg Ct NN18 8 D2
Brighouse Cl NN18 8 D2
Brighton Rd NN18 8 B2
Brightwell Walk NN9 26 B2
Brigstock Rd NN14 11 B4
Brindley Cl NN10 32 C1
Brington Dr NN15 17 F5
Brinkhill Walk*, Boston Cl NN18 8 D2
Brinsley Grn NN18 6 B6
Brisbane Gdns NN18 8 C4
Britannia Gdns NN8 30 C1
Britannia Rd NN16 14 B3
Britannia Walk LE16 5 D6
British La*, School La NN16 3 C4
Brixham Walk*, Burghley Dr NN18 9 G1
Broad St NN6 34 B3
Broadlands, Kettering NN14 12 D4
Broadlands, Rushden NN10 33 F2
Broadlands, Wellingborough NN9 21 G3
Broadstone Ct NN18 6 A6
Broadway, Kettering NN15 16 C1
Broadway, Wellingborough NN8 30 A2
Broadway Ter*, The Crescent LE16 4 D4
Brockhill Cl NN15 17 E1
Bronte Cl NN16 14 D1
Brook Haven NN14 19 C5
Brook St NN9 21 G3
Brook St East NN8 30 B1
Brook St West NN8 29 H1
Brook Ter NN9 36 B3
Brook Vale NN8 29 F4
Brooke Cl, Rushden NN10 33 E4
Brooke Cl, Wellingborough NN8 23 E6
Brooke Mews NN8 23 E6
Brooke Rd NN18 8 C5
Brookes Gro NN17 7 E3
Brookes Mews NN6 34 B2
Brookfield Rd, Market Harborough LE16 5 A5
Brookfield Rd, Rushden NN10 32 D3
Brooklands Gdns LE16 5 C6
Brooks Cl NN15 18 E3
Brooks Rd NN9 21 H2
Brooksdale Cl NN16 14 C2
Brookside, Kettering NN14 12 D4
Brookside, Wellingborough NN9 20 D6
Broom Way NN15 13 D6
Broughton By-Pass NN14 19 A6
Broughton Rd NN18 9 E4
Browning Av NN16 14 D2
Browning Rd NN8 29 E1
Browning Walk*, Wordsworth Av NN17 6 D3
Brunel Cl, Kettering NN16 14 B4
Brunel Cl, Wellingborough NN8 23 E4
Brunel Ct NN17 7 G2
Brunel Rd NN17 7 F2

Brunswick Gdns NN18 8 A4
Bryant Rd NN15 16 D4
Bryant Way NN10 27 E5
Buccleuch St NN16 14 B5
Buckfast Sq NN18 9 G2
Buckingham Cl NN8 29 H4
Buckingham Ct NN15 17 G3
Buckwell Cl, Kettering NN14 12 C3
Buckwell Cl, Wellingborough NN8 23 H6
Buckwell End NN8 23 H6
Buckwell Pl NN8 29 H1
Bugby Dr NN9 36 D1
Bugby Way NN9 21 G2
Bunting Cl NN15 18 C3
Burditt Cl NN14 19 D2
Burford Way NN8 29 F4
Burgess Ct NN18 8 B2
Burghley Cl, Corby NN18 9 F2
Burghley Cl, Kettering NN14 12 C2
Burghley Cl, Market Harborough LE16 5 E6
Burghley Dr NN18 3 C3
Burghley St NN16 14 C3
Burkitt Rd NN17 7 E1
Burleigh Ho*, Rectory Ct NN10 33 E3
Burnmill Rd LE16 4 C4
Burns Cl NN6 34 C4
Burns Dr NN17 6 C4
Burns Rd, Kettering NN16 14 D2
Burns Rd, Wellingborough NN8 29 E1
Burton Latimer By-Pass NN15 18 F1
Burton Rd NN9 22 B1
Burtone Cl NN14 19 B5
Bury Cl, Kettering NN16 11 C1
Bury Cl, Rushden NN10 27 F5
Burystead Pl NN8 30 A1
Burystead Rise NN9 21 G2
Bush Acre Ct NN16 13 D2
Bush Cl NN8 23 H6
Bushey Bank Cl NN18 8 C5
Bute Cl NN17 6 B4
Butland Rd NN18 8 D4
Butler Gdns LE16 5 A8
Butlin Cl NN14 19 A2
Butlin Ct NN8 30 C4
Butterfields NN8 30 A3
Buttermere NN8 23 F6
Buttermere Cl NN16 13 C3
Butterwick Walk*, Boston Cl NN18 8 D2
Butts Rd, Raunds NN9 21 G2
Butts Rd, Wellingborough NN8 29 H4
Buxton Dr NN14 12 A2
Byron Cres, Rushden NN10 32 C3
Byron Cres, Warmonds Hill NN10 27 E6
Byron Rd, Corby NN17 6 C4
Byron Rd, Kettering NN16 14 D3
Byron Rd, Wellingborough NN8 29 F1

Cabot Cl NN14 19 C2
Calder Cl NN17 6 C2
Callcott Dr NN15 17 G2
Calvert Cl NN8 23 H3
Cam Cl NN17 6 C2
Cambium Cl NN16 14 D1
Cambridge Av NN17 6 B6
Cambridge St, Kettering NN14 19 B1
Cambridge St, Rothwell NN16 14 D4
Cambridge St, Rushden NN10 33 E6
Cambridge St, Wellingborough NN8 24 A6
Cameron Ct NN17 3 C3
Campbell Rd, Corby NN17 3 C2
Campbell Rd, Wellingborough NN8 30 A3
Campbell Sq NN6 34 A3
Campion Cl NN10 33 F5
Camsdale Walk NN16 11 C2
Canada Sq NN18 8 D3
Cannam Cl NN16 11 B1
Cannock Rd NN17 7 E4
Cannon St NN8 24 B6
Canon St NN16 14 C5
Canonbury NN8 29 E1
Cantle Cl NN18 9 E3
Capell Gdns NN18 9 F2
Cardigan Pl, Corby NN17 3 B2
Cardigan Pl, Kettering NN16 15 E5
Cardigan Rd NN14 11 B5
Carey Dr NN17 6 C4
Carey St NN16 14 D5
Carey Way NN10 33 G2
Carina Rd NN15 16 D5
Carisbrooke Cl NN15 17 G2
Carlton Cl NN10 33 E6
Carlton Mews NN10 27 F6
Carlton Pl NN18 6 B6
Carlton St NN16 14 B5
Carmarthen Way NN10 33 G5
Carnegie St NN10 33 E3
Carradale Cl NN16 14 B2
Carriage Dr NN16 14 C1
Carrington St NN16 3 C4
Carron Cl NN17 6 C2
Carsington Cl NN16 13 C3
Carter Av NN14 19 B6
Carter Cl NN8 30 B1
Cartmel Way NN10 33 G2
Cartrill St NN9 21 F3
Casterton Cl NN9 20 D4
Castle Cl NN18 8 B2
Castle Ct, Rushden NN10 33 E5
Castle Ct, Wellingborough NN8 30 B1
Castle Flds NN8 30 C1
Castle Hill NN14 19 B2
Castle La NN8 30 B1
Castle Mews NN8 30 B1
Castle Rd NN8 30 B1
Castle St NN8 30 B1
Castle Way, Kettering NN15 17 F3
Castle Way, Wellingborough NN8 30 B1
Castleton Rd NN14 12 A2
Catchland Cl NN18 8 D5
Catchpole Cl NN18 9 E3
Catesby Rd NN14 19 D2
Catesby St NN16 14 D5
Causeway Rd NN17 6 D2
Cavendish Cl NN15 17 G4
Cavendish Courtyard NN17 10 C2
Caxton St LE16 5 D7
Caythorpe Sq NN18 6 B6
Cecil Cl NN18 9 F2
Cecil Dr NN18 9 F2
Cecil St, Kettering NN16 14 C3
Cecil St, Rothwell NN14 19 C1
Cedar Cl, Kettering NN14 12 E3
Cedar Cl, Rushden NN10 33 E5
Cedar Cl, Wellingborough NN29 31 G6
Cedar Ct NN17 6 D3
Cedar Rd NN16 14 D4
Cedar Way, Rushden NN10 27 E4
Cedar Way, Wellingborough NN8 24 A4
Celandine Cl NN10 33 G6
Cemetery La NN10 27 F5
Centaine Rd NN10 32 D4
Central Av, Kettering NN16 15 E5
Central Av, Wellingborough NN8 29 G3
Centre Par NN16 15 E4
Chace Rd NN8 30 C1
Chamberlain Av NN8 29 H4
Chamberlain Way, Rushden NN10 27 F6
Chamberlain Way, Wellingborough NN9 21 F4
Chandlers Way NN17 3 B3
Channing St NN16 3 D4
Chapel Hill, Rushden NN10 27 F3
Chapel Hill, Wellingborough NN29 31 G5
Chapel La, Corby NN17 7 G5
Chapel La, Stanwick NN9 20 D6
Chapel La, Wellingborough NN29 35 G1
Chapel Rd NN17 10 D3
Chapel Vw NN14 19 B4
Chaplins La NN14 12 D3
Chapman Gro NN17 7 E4
Chapmans Cl NN29 31 H6
Charlbury Cl NN8 29 H5
Charles Cl NN10 27 F4
Charles Partridge Ct NN8 29 E4
Charles Robinson Ct NN8 29 G2
Charles St, Corby NN17 3 C3
Charles St, Kettering NN16 14 B4
Charles St, Rothwell NN14 19 A2
Charles St, Market Harborough LE16 5 A6
Charles St, Wellingborough NN8 29 G3
Charlotte Pl NN16 15 F4
Charnwood Dr NN15 17 G5
Charnwood Rd NN17 7 E5
Chase Cl NN14 11 B5
Chaston Pl NN16 15 E3
Chatellebault Ct NN17 6 D4
Chater Cl LE16 4 E2
Chatsworth Av NN15 16 D5
Chatsworth Dr, Market Harborough LE16 5 E5
Chatsworth Dr, Wellingborough NN8 23 E4
Chaucer Rd NN8 29 F1
Cheddar Walk NN18 6 A6
Cheese La*, The Swansgate Centre NN8 30 A1
Chelmorton Vale NN14 12 A2
Cheltenham Cl NN10 33 G5
Chelveston Dr NN17 6 B5
Chelveston Rd, Raunds NN9 21 F4
Chelveston Rd, Rushden NN10 27 G5
Chelveston Rd, Stanwick NN9 20 D6
Chepstow Cl NN15 17 F2
Chepstow Dr NN8 23 E4
Chequers La NN8 24 A6
Cheriton Rd NN18 9 G2
Cherradene Ct NN9 21 G3
Cherry Av NN8 24 A4
Cherry Ct NN9 36 A5
Cherry Orchard NN10 33 F4
Cherry Rd NN16 14 D3
Cherry St NN9 36 A5
Cherry Tree Cl NN14 12 D3
Cherry Way NN9 21 E4
Cherwell Walk NN17 6 C2
Chesil Walk NN18 6 A5
Chester Ct NN15 16 C3
Chester Ho NN8 31 F3
Chester Rd, Irchester NN29 31 G3
Chester Rd, Rushden NN10 32 C4
Chester Rd, Wellingborough NN8 30 C1
Chestnut Av, Corby NN17 6 D3
Chestnut Av, Kettering NN15 3 D6
Chestnut Cl NN10 32 D2
Chestnut Dr NN14 12 E3
Chestnut Gro NN15 16 D2
Cheviot Cl NN16 14 C1
Cheyne Walk NN15 17 E2
Chichele Cl NN10 27 F5
Chichele Ct NN10 33 E2
Chichele St NN10 27 F5
Chichester Cl NN14 19 D2
Chieftan Bsns Centre NN8 22 D5
Chiltern Cl LE16 4 C3
Chiltern Rd NN16 14 B2
Chowns Mill Bsns Pk NN9 36 D6
Christie Way NN15 16 A2
Christine Ct NN9 21 G3
Church Dr NN18 8 C6
Church Hall Rd NN10 32 C4
Church Hill NN9 22 A2
Church La, Great Doddington NN29 35 G1
Church La, Kettering NN15 18 E2
Church La, Wilby NN8 29 E4
Church La, Wollaston NN29 35 F4
Church Sq*, Church St LE16 5 C5
Church St, Broughton NN14 19 B5
Church St, Burton Latimer NN15 18 E2
Church St, Corby NN17 10 E4
Church St, Cottingham NN16 11 C1
Church St, Finedon NN9 22 B2
Church St, Irthlingborough NN9 36 B4
Church St, Isham NN14 18 B4
Church St, Market Harborough LE16 5 C5
Church St, Raunds NN9 21 G2
Church St, Rushden NN10 33 E3
Church St, Stanwick NN9 20 C6
Church St, Wellingborough NN8 30 A1
Church View Rd NN14 12 D3
Church Vw, Broughton NN14 19 B5
Church Vw, Burton Latimer NN15 18 E2
Church Vw, Corby NN17 10 E3
Church Vw, Wellingborough NN9 21 G2
Church Walk, Corby NN17 7 G6
Church Walk, Kettering NN16 3 C5
Church Walk, Weldon NN17 10 E3
Church Walk, Wellingborough NN9 36 B4
Church Way NN8 30 A1
Churchill Av, Irthlingborough NN9 36 D1
Churchill Av, Wellingborough NN8 23 G4
Churchill Cl NN14 19 C2
Churchill Rd NN6 34 B3
Churchill Way, Barton Seagrave NN15 17 F1
Churchill Way, Burton Latimer NN15 18 D3
Clare Cl NN6 34 C4
Clare Rd NN8 29 F2
Clare St NN9 21 G3
Clare Walk NN10 27 E6
Claremont Dr LE16 5 E5
Clarence Ct NN10 32 D5
Clarence Rd NN16 14 D5
Clarence St LE16 5 D5
Clarke Cl, Kettering NN16 14 B4
Clarke Cl, Wellingborough NN9 36 D2
Clarke Ct NN6 34 C3
Clarke Rd NN17 6 D4
Clarke St LE16 5 B5
Claydon Cl NN8 23 H6
Cleaver Ct NN15 3 B6
Cleburne Cl, Raunds NN9 21 E4
Cleburne Cl, Stanwick NN9 20 D5
Cleeve Way NN8 29 G4
Cleveland Av NN16 14 B1
Clifton Cl NN15 16 D1
Clifton Gro NN15 16 D1
Clifton Sq NN17 7 E4
Clipstone Ct NN14 19 B2
Clipstone St LE16 5 D7
Clive Cl NN15 17 F1
Clovelly Ct NN18 9 G2
Clover Dr NN10 33 F5
Clover Gdns NN16 14 B4
Club St NN16 14 C5
Clun Walk NN17 6 C2
Clwyd Walk NN17 6 C2
Clydesdale Rd NN17 6 D4
Coales Gdns LE16 4 B3
Coalport Cl NN14 12 B3
Cobb's La NN29 35 E5
Cobden St NN16 14 B5
Cockerell Rd NN17 7 G4
Cockerwood Cl NN18 8 C5
Coffee Tavern Ct NN10 33 E3
Coffee Tavern La NN10 33 F3
Cogan Cres NN14 19 A2
Coggins Cl NN9 21 F3
Coldermeadow Av NN18 8 B3
Cole Ct NN9 21 F3
Cole St NN10 32 C1
Coleman St NN9 21 G3
Coleridge Way NN17 6 C4
College St, Higham Ferrers NN10 27 F5
College St, Irthlingborough NN9 36 A4
College St, Rushden NN10 33 E3
College St, Wellingborough NN8 29 H1
College St, Wollaston NN29 35 F5
Collingham Cl NN9 20 D4
Collingwood Av NN17 6 A5
Colne Cl NN17 6 C2
Coltsfoot Rd NN10 33 G6
Columbus Cres NN14 19 C2
Colwell Rd NN8 30 C1
Colyers Av NN18 8 C2
Comfrey Cl NN10 33 F6
Commercial Rd, Corby NN17 7 H6
Commercial Rd, Kettering NN16 3 B4
Commercial St NN10 27 E6
Commercial Way NN8 30 A1
Compton Cl NN6 34 B5
Compton Pl NN16 15 E5
Compton Rd NN8 24 C6
Compton Way NN6 34 B4
Coniston Cl, Rushden NN10 27 E3
Coniston Cl, Wellingborough NN8 23 E6
Coniston Rd NN16 13 D4
Connaught Rd LE16 5 D5
Connaught St NN16 14 D4
Connell Ct NN17 3 C3
Connolly Cl NN14 19 D2
Connolly Dr NN14 19 D1
Constable Dr, Kettering NN15 17 G2
Constable Dr, Wellingborough NN8 23 H3
Constable Rd NN18 3 A3
Conway Cl, Rushden NN10 33 E5
Conway Cl, Wellingborough NN8 23 F5
Conway Dr NN15 18 D3
Conway Walk NN17 6 C2
Cook Cl NN14 19 C2
Cooks Rd NN17 10 C2
Cooper Dr NN8 23 H3
Co-Operative Row NN10 33 F4
Copelands Rd NN14 12 E2
Copenhagen Rd NN18 8 A5
Copperfield Cl NN16 14 C2
Coppice Cl NN15 18 E1
Copse Cl NN15 18 E1
Cora Rd NN16 15 E4
Corby Rd, Corby NN17 10 C3
Corby Rd, Cottingham NN16 11 D1
Corby Rd, Stanion NN14 11 B5
Cordon Cres NN6 34 C3
Corn La*, The Swansgate Centre NN8 30 A1
Cornfield Way NN15 18 E3
Cornwall Cl NN17 6 B6
Cornwall Rd NN16 14 D5
Coronation Av, Kettering NN14 19 C2
Coronation Av, Rushden NN10 32 C4
Corporation St NN17 3 B2
Corts Yd*, Roman Way LE16 5 C5
Cotswold Av NN16 14 B3
Cotswold Dr NN8 29 F4
Cottesbrooke Rd NN17 6 B5
Cottesmore Av NN15 17 G5
Cottesmore Way NN8 29 G1
Cottingham Rd NN17 3 A1
Coulon Cl NN29 31 G6
Council St NN29 35 F6
Counts Farm Rd NN18 9 F2
Courier Rd NN17 7 G5
Court Dr NN16 14 C2
Court Mews NN8 30 B1
Courtman Rd NN9 20 D4
Courtney Rd NN10 32 D4
Courtwood NN9 20 D6
Coventry Rd LE16 5 A6
Covington Gro NN8 24 A5
Cowper Cl, Northampton NN6 34 C3
Cowper Cl, Wellingborough NN9 26 B2
Cowper Rd NN8 29 F1
Cowper St NN16 14 C3
Cowslip Cl NN10 33 F5
Coxs La NN14 19 B4
Crabb St NN10 33 F4
Crabtree Cl NN8 29 H3
Craddock Ct NN29 31 (
Cragside NN8 23
Craigie NN8 29
Crane Cl, Rushden NN10 33
Crane Cl, Wellingborough NN8 30
Cranford Rd, Barton Seagrave NN15 17
Cranford Rd, Burton Latimer NN15 18
Cranleigh Ho*, Rectory Ct NN10 33
Cranleigh Rd NN15 16
Cransley Gdns NN17 6
Cransley Hill NN14 19
Crawford Gro NN17 6 [
Crawley Av NN8 23 C
Creighton Cres NN15 17
Crescent Cl LE16 4 [
Cresswell Rd NN10 32 [
Cresswell Walk NN17 6 C
Crick Cl NN17 7
Cricketers Grn NN17 10
Crispin Pl NN16 3 E
Crispin St, Burton Latimer NN15 18 E
Crispin St, Rothwell NN14 19 C
Crocus Way NN10 33
Croft Cl NN8 23 E
Croft Way NN10 33 G
Cromarty Ct NN17 3 C
Cromer Rd NN9 22 E
Cromwell Cl NN14 12 C
Cromwell Cres LE16 5 E
Cromwell Ct NN8 24 E
Cromwell Rd, Kettering NN16 3 A
Cromwell Rd, Rushden NN10 33 F
Cronin Courtyard NN18 10 B
Cronin Rd NN18 10 B
Crosby Rd LE16 5 D
Cross Rd NN8 24 E
Cross St, Kettering NN16 14 E
Cross St, Market Harborough LE16 5 C
Cross St, Rothwell NN14 19 C
Cross Way NN9 26 E
Crouch Rd NN9 36 E
Crown Ct, Corby NN17 3 B
Crown Ct, Rushden NN10 32 C
Crown La NN14 19 B
Crown St NN16 14 C
Crown Way NN10 32 C
Croxen Cl NN15 18 E
Croyde Av NN18 9 F
Croyland Ct NN8 29 H
Croyland Rd NN8 29 H
Crucible Rd NN17 7 G
Culloden Ct NN17 3 C
Culloden Dr NN15 17 F
Culross Walk NN18 8 D
Cumberland Av NN9 20 D
Cunliffe Dr NN16 14 B
Cunningham Cl NN10 27 E
Cupar Cres NN17 3 C
Curtis Mews NN8 23 F
Curver Way NN17 10 B
Cypress Cl NN14 12 B
Cytringan Cl NN15 16 B

Daffodil Dr NN10 33 F
Dahlia Rd NN16 14 D
Dairy Way NN9 26 B
Daisy Bank Av NN14 19 A
Daisy Cft NN10 33 F
Dalby Cl NN16 14 B
Dale Av NN8 23 E
Dale Cl NN8 23 E
Dale Ho*, Wood St NN8 30 A
Dale St, Corby NN17 6 D
Dale St, Wellingborough NN8 29 H
Dalkeith Av NN16 3 C
Dalkeith Mews NN16 3 B
Dalkeith Pl NN16 3 C
Dalkeith Rd NN8 29 H
Dallison Cl LE16 5 C
Dalton Rd NN17 6 D
Dance Way NN8 24 A
Dando Cl NN29 35 F
Danesholme Rd NN18 8 A
Daniels Rd NN8 30 C
Darby Cl NN8 22 C
Darescroft NN16 11 B
Darley Cl NN16 14 D
Darley Dale NN17 6 D4
Dart Cl NN17 6 D2
Darwin Rd NN17 7 H3
Dash Farm Cl NN17 10 D3
Davey Rd NN17 7 H4
Davies Cl NN15 13 D6
Davis Cl NN14 19 C2
Davis Ct NN17 7 G6
Davy Cl NN8 22 D5
Dawkins Ct*, High St NN14 19 B5
Dayton St NN10 32 D3
De Ferneus Dr NN9 21 G2
Deacon Cl, Market Harborough LE16 4 B3
Deacon Cl, Rushden NN10 33 G2
Dean Cl NN10 32 D5
Debdale Rd NN8 23 H6
Debdale Spring Fm NN29 35 E3
Deben Rd NN17 6 D2
Deeble Rd NN15 15 E6
Deene Cl, Corby NN17 7 E5
Deene Cl, Market Harborough LE16 5 E5

Deene End NN17 10 F3
Deeneside NN17 10 E3
Delamere Dr NN15 17 G5
Delapre Pl NN18 8 B3
Delisle Cl LE16 5 B7
Dell Pl NN10 33 F3
Dempsey Dr NN14 19 D2
Denbeigh Ho*, Rectory Ct NN10 33 E3
Denby Dale NN8 23 F4
Dencora Bsns Pk NN8 28 D1
Dene Cl, Kettering NN16 14 B2
Dene Cl, Wellingborough NN8 23 F5
Denford Dr NN15 17 F5
Denford Rd NN17 6 B4
Denford Way NN8 23 F4
Denington Ct NN8 30 B3
Denington Ind Est NN8 30 B3
Denington Rd NN8 30 A3
Denmark Cl NN18 8 A3
Denmark Ct NN10 33 F4
Denmark Rd NN10 33 F4
Denne Cl NN18 8 D5
Denton Cl, Rushden NN10 33 F2
Denton Cl, Wellingborough NN29 31 H5
Denton Ct NN15 18 E2
Derling Dr NN9 21 H2
Derwent Cl NN8 23 E5
Derwent Cres NN16 14 A6
Derwent Walk NN17 6 D2
Desborough Rd NN14 19 A1
Deveron Walk NN17 6 D2
Devon Dr NN15 16 D4
Devon Walk NN10 33 F4
Devonshire Cl NN8 23 G5
Diamond Dr NN9 26 B2
Diana Way NN15 18 D3
Dickens Dr NN16 14 C2
Digby St NN16 14 C5
Dingle Rd NN10 32 B3
Dingley Rd LE16 4 F2
Dingley Ter LE16 5 D5
Ditchford Rd NN8 25 H4
Dixon Walk*, High St NN17 7 G6
Doctors La NN29 35 G1
Doddington Rd, Northampton NN6 34 B3
Doddington Rd, Wellingborough NN8 30 A4
Doddington Rd, Wilby NN8 28 D5
Doddridge Rd LE16 5 C5
Dolben Av NN9 20 C5
Dolben Cl NN9 22 A3
Dolben Sq NN9 22 B2
Dolver Cl NN18 8 D5
Don Cl NN17 6 C2
Donaldson Av NN14 19 B6
Donne Cl, Kettering NN16 14 D2
Donne Cl, Rushden NN10 26 D6
Doris Rd NN16 15 E4
Dorking Walk NN18 8 D3
Dorothy Rd NN16 15 E5
Dorset Rd NN17 6 B6
Douglas Ct NN15 17 F1
Douglas Dr LE16 4 D4
Doulton Cl NN14 12 B3
Dovecote Cl, Kettering NN15 17 G2
Dovecote Cl, Wellingborough NN9 21 G2
Dovedale NN14 12 A2
Dovedale Rd NN17 6 D5
Dovehouse Cl NN9 20 C6
Dover Cl NN10 33 G4
Dowthorpe End NN6 34 B3
Dowthorpe Hill NN6 34 B4
Drake Cl, Corby NN17 6 A4
Drake Cl, Kettering NN14 19 D1
Drake Lee Mews*, St Peters Av NN16 3 C6
Drayton Cl, Corby NN18 8 B2
Drayton Cl, Rushden NN10 32 D5
Drayton Pl NN9 36 B3
Drayton Rd NN9 36 B3
Dresden Cl NN18 8 A5
Driffield Gro NN17 7 F5
Drill Hall Ct NN15 3 A6
Droue Ct NN14 19 B2
Dryden Rd NN8 24 C6
Dryden St, Kettering NN16 14 B5
Dryden St, Wellingborough NN9 21 F3
Dryden Way, Corby NN17 6 C4
Dryden Way, Rushden NN10 27 E6
Dryland St NN16 3 B4
Duchess Cl NN16 14 C4
Duchy Cl NN10 27 F6
Duck End NN29 35 F4
Duck St NN10 33 E3
Duckworth Rd NN17 6 A5
Duke St, Burton Latimer NN15 18 D3
Duke St, Kettering NN16 14 B4
Duke St, Wellingborough NN8 29 G3
Dulley Av NN8 29 H4
Dumble Cl NN18 8 D3
Dunbar Ct NN15 17 F1
Duncan Ct NN8 29 G3
Duncan Rd NN17 6 B5
Dunedin Rd NN18 8 C4
Dunkirk Av NN14 12 C3
Dunslade Cl LE16 5 F6
Dunslade Gro LE16 5 F6
Dunslade Rd LE16 5 E6
Durban Rd NN16 14 D6
Durham Cl NN17 6 B6
Durness Cl NN15 17 E2
Dybdale Cres NN8 23 G6
Dyson Dr NN16 14 B4
Eady Rd NN15 18 D3
Ealing Ter NN10 33 E2
Earls Barton Rd NN29 35 E3
Earlstress Ind Est NN17 7 E2
Earlstress Rd NN17 7 E3
East Av, Burton Latimer NN15 18 D2
East Av, Corby NN17 3 D3
East Av, Kettering NN15 15 E6
East Carlton Pk NN16 11 A3
East Cl NN15 15 E6
East Cres, Corby NN17 10 F3
East Cres, Rushden NN10 32 C3
East Dr NN15 15 E6
East Gro NN10 33 E2
East Langham Rd NN9 21 G2
East St, Irchester NN29 31 G5
East St, Market Harborough LE16 5 B5
East St, Stanwick NN9 20 D6
East Walk NN15 15 E6
Eastbourne Av NN18 8 C1
Eastbrook NN18 8 C2
Eastbrook Hill NN14 12 F3
Eastfield Cres NN9 22 C1
Eastfield Rd, Irthlingborough NN9 36 B4
Eastfield Rd, Wellingborough NN8 24 C5
Eastfield Rd, Wollaston NN29 35 F5
Eastlands Rd NN9 22 C1
Eastleigh Rd NN15 17 E2
Easton Walk*, High St NN17 7 G6
Ebbw Vale Rd NN9 26 B2
Ebenezer Pl NN16 3 B4
Edale Grn NN14 12 A2
Eden St NN16 14 C5
Edgar Rd NN10 15 E5
Edgell St NN16 3 D4
Edinburgh Cl, Kettering NN14 19 A3
Edinburgh Cl, Market Harborough LE16 5 D5
Edinburgh Rd, Kettering NN16 14 D5
Edinburgh Rd, Wellingborough NN8 29 G4
Edison Cl NN8 22 C5
Edison Courtyard NN17 7 F1
Edison Ct NN8 22 C5
Edith Rd NN16 15 F3
Edmonds Cl NN8 30 B4
Edmund St NN16 14 D5
Edward Cl, Kettering NN15 16 D3
Edward Cl, Rushden NN10 27 G4
Edward Rd, Kettering NN15 16 D3
Edward Rd, Market Harborough LE16 4 B4
Edward Rd, Wellingborough NN29 31 H6
Edwards Dr NN8 23 G6
Eider Cl NN15 18 C2
Eismann Way NN17 7 H4
Elan Ct NN10 32 C2
Eliot Cl NN16 14 D2
Eliot Way NN10 27 E6
Elizabeth Cl, Northampton NN6 34 B2
Elizabeth Cl, Wellingborough NN8 29 G3
Elizabeth Ct NN10 27 G4
Elizabeth Rd, Kettering NN16 15 E5
Elizabeth Rd, Rothwell NN14 19 B3
Elizabeth St NN17 3 B2
Elizabeth Way, Northampton NN6 34 A2
Elizabeth Way, Rushden NN10 27 F3
Elizabeth Way, Wellingborough NN9 26 C3
Ellison Cl NN9 21 F2
Elm Dr LE16 5 A6
Elm Rd, Burton Latimer NN15 18 E1
Elm Rd, Kettering NN15 14 D6
Elm St NN8 23 H5
Elm Walk NN10 27 E5
Elsden Rd NN8 24 C6
Ennerdale Cl NN16 14 A6
Ennerdale Rd, Corby NN17 6 D3
Ennerdale Rd, Rushden NN10 33 G2
Ensleigh Cl NN15 18 E3
Enstone Ct NN8 29 G4
Enterprise Cl NN16 13 D2
Enterprise Ct NN8 22 D5
Enterprise Rd NN9 21 G2
Epping Cl NN15 17 G5
Epsom Cl NN10 33 G5
Epsom Walk NN18 8 C3
Eskdaill St NN16 14 C5
Eskdale Av NN17 7 E5
Eskdale Cl NN8 23 F5
Essex Cl NN17 6 B6
Essex Gdns LE16 5 B7
Essex Pl NN15 16 D4
Essex Rd NN10 33 F4
Ettrick Cl NN16 14 B2
Euro Bsns Pk LE16 4 F4
Evelyn Way NN29 32 A6
Evensford Walk NN9 26 B3
Everest La NN17 3 B2
Everitt Cl NN8 30 B3
Evesham Cl NN8 29 G4
Evison Rd NN14 19 B2
Ewenfield Rd NN9 22 B3
Excelsior NN8 29 E1
Excelsior Ct NN9 36 A4
Exeter St NN16 14 C3
Exmouth Av NN18 9 G2
Express Cl NN9 26 B3
Express Pk NN10 32 A2
Eyam Cl NN14 12 A2
Factory La*, Church St LE16 5 C5
Fairfax Rd LE16 5 C7
Fairfield Rd, Kettering NN14 18 A4
Fairfield Rd, Market Harborough LE16 5 B5
Fairhurst Walk*, Ashurst Cres NN18 8 C1
Fairhurst Way NN6 34 B3
Fairmead Cres NN10 32 D5
Fairoaks Dr NN9 21 F2
Fairway LE16 4 B4
Fallowfield NN8 23 H3
Falmer Walk*, Farmstead Rd NN18 8 C2
Falster Cl NN18 8 B4
Faraday Cl NN8 22 D4
Faraday Ct NN8 22 C5
Faraday Gro NN17 7 F4
Farm Rd NN8 23 H3
Farmfield Cl NN15 17 G6
Farmstead Rd NN18 8 B1
Farnborough Cl NN15 16 D5
Farndale Av NN17 6 D5
Farndish Cl NN10 32 C3
Farndish Rd NN29 31 G5
Farndon Rd LE16 5 A8
Farnham Dr NN10 32 D5
Feast Field Cl NN29 35 F6
Featherbed La NN18 9 H4
Federation Av NN14 12 B4
Fell Walk NN8 23 F5
Fellows Cl NN29 35 E5
Fenners Cl NN10 33 G3
Fermyn Pl NN18 8 B3
Fern Ley Cl LE16 5 F6
Fern Rd NN10 32 B3
Fernfield Cl LE16 5 F5
Fernie Cl NN15 17 G4
Fernie Rd LE16 5 D5
Fernie Way NN8 29 G2
Fernmoor Dr NN9 36 B4
Ferrers Ct NN10 27 G4
Ferrestone Rd NN8 24 A5
Fettledine Rd NN9 36 D1
Field Cotts NN18 8 C6
Field St NN16 14 B5
Field St Av NN16 14 B5
Fieldhead Cl LE16 5 A5
Fields Vw NN8 30 B1
Finch Dr NN15 17 G4
Finedon Rd, Irthlingborough NN9 36 A3
Finedon Rd, Kettering NN15 18 D4
Finedon Rd, Wellingborough NN8 24 B6
Finedon Rd Ind Est NN8 24 B2
Finedon St NN15 18 D3
Fineshade Cl NN15 17 G5
Fineshade Gro NN17 7 E4
Finland Way NN18 8 B4
Fir Rd NN16 14 D6
Fir Tree Walk LE16 5 C5
Firdale Av NN10 33 F1
First Av NN8 29 F3
Fishton Cl NN15 16 C3
Fitzwilliam Dr NN15 17 G4
Fitzwilliam Leys NN10 27 E4
Fitzwilliam Rd NN9 36 B3
Fitzwilliam St NN10 33 E3
Flaxland Cl LE16 5 F6
Fleet St NN16 3 A4
Fleetwood Cl LE16 5 B7
Fleetwood Gdns LE16 5 A7
Fleming Cl NN8 22 C4
Fleming Rd NN17 7 F2
Flensburg Cl NN18 8 B4
Fletcher Rd NN10 33 E2
Ford St NN16 3 D4
Forest Cl NN15 18 F1
Forest Ct NN10 33 G2
Forest Gate Rd NN17 3 B1
Forest Glade NN16 14 D1
Forge Ho*, High St NN14 19 B2
Foskett Cl NN10 33 E2
Fosse Cl NN8 29 G4
Fosse Grn NN10 33 G2
Fosse Rd NN18 8 B5
Foster Cl NN15 13 D5
Foster Ct NN18 9 F1
Fothergill Cl LE16 5 F6
Fotheringhay Rd NN17 6 B4
Fourth Av NN8 29 F2
Fowey Cl NN8 23 E5
Fox St NN14 19 B2
Fox Yd*, Church St LE16 5 C5
Foxglove Cl NN10 33 F5
Foxlands NN14 12 D4
Foxton Ct NN15 16 B1
Foxwood Cl NN10 32 C3
Francis Ct NN10 32 B2
Francis Ct NN10 32 C1
Francis Dickins Cl NN29 35 G5
Francis St NN9 21 E4
Francis Ter NN9 21 E4
Franciscan Cl NN10 32 D5
Franklin Flds NN17 7 G4
Freeman Way NN9 22 D2
French Dr NN15 17 F1
Friars Cl NN8 30 A2
Frinton Cl NN10 32 D5
Frost Ct NN29 35 G1
Fuchsia Way NN10 33 F6
Fuller St NN16 14 D5
Fulmar La NN8 24 A3
Furlong Rd NN14 12 E3
Furnace La NN16 13 D1
Furnells Cl NN9 21 G2
Fyfe Rd NN17 6 B3
Gainage Cl NN18 8 D4
Gainsborough Av NN15 17 G3
Gainsborough Ct NN18 9 E1
Gainsborough Dr NN8 23 H4
Gainsborough Rd NN18 8 B3
Gamston Walk*, Beanfield Av NN18 6 B6
Gander Cl NN17 10 E3
Gannet La NN8 24 B3
Garden Fields Cl NN9 36 D1
Garden Fields Ct NN29 31 H5
Gardenfield NN10 27 E6
Gardiner St LE16 5 A5
Gardner Cl NN9 21 F2
Garfield St NN15 16 C1
Garrard Way NN16 13 D3
Garrow Cl NN9 36 A3
Garston Rd NN18 8 D5
Gate La NN14 19 C4
Gateford Ct NN18 6 B6
Gates Cl NN9 36 A3
Geddington Rd NN18 7 H6
Genner Rd NN17 7 H3
Gentian Cl NN10 33 F5
George Blackhall Ct*, Rowlett Rd NN17 6 B4
George St, Burton Latimer NN15 18 F1
George St, Corby NN17 3 A1
George St, Higham Ferrers NN10 27 F4
George St, Irthlingborough NN9 36 A5
George St, Kettering NN16 3 B5
George St, Rushden NN10 33 E3
George St, Wellingborough NN8 24 A6
Gerrard Gdns LE16 5 B8
Gharana Nivas NN8 24 B6
Gibbons Dr NN14 19 D2
Gilbert Cl LE16 5 F6
Gilbey Cl NN9 23 H2
Gilchrist Av NN17 7 F4
Gillingham Rd NN15 13 D6
Gillitts Rd NN8 29 G2
Gipsy La, Kettering NN16 13 C2
Gipsy La, Wellingborough NN29 30 C5
Gisburne Rd NN8 24 B5
Glade Cl NN15 18 E2
Gladstone Ct*, Gladstone St NN16 3 D4
Gladstone St, Desborough NN14 12 C2
Gladstone St, Kettering NN16 3 D4
Gladstone St, Market Harborough LE16 5 D7
Gladstone St, Rothwell NN14 19 B1
Gladstone Ter NN9 21 G3
Glaister Pl NN16 15 E5
Glamis Cl NN10 33 G4
Glassbrook Rd NN10 32 D3
Glastonbury Cl NN15 17 F2
Glastonbury Rd NN18 6 A6
Glebe Av, Broughton NN14 19 C5
Glebe Av, Kettering NN15 16 C2
Glebe Farm Ct NN29 35 G1
Glebe Rd, Kettering NN15 18 C2
Glebe Rd, Market Harborough LE16 5 E6
Glen Bank NN8 30 B1
Glencoe Dr NN15 17 F1
Glendon Rd NN14 19 C2
Gleneagles Cl NN15 17 F1
Gleneagles Dr NN8 23 F3
Glenfield Cl NN10 32 C2
Glenfield Dr NN29 35 F2
Glenmore Cl NN16 14 B1
Glenshee Cl NN15 17 E2
Gloucester Cl NN16 3 D4
Gloucester Cres NN10 33 F2
Gloucester Ct NN14 19 B2
Gloucester Pl NN8 30 A1
Glyndebourne Gdns NN18 8 B2
Goadbys Yd*, Church Walk NN16 3 C6
Godwin Rd NN17 7 F1
Gold End NN16 14 B5
Gold St, Desborough NN14 12 C2
Gold St, Kettering NN16 3 B4
Gold St, Wellingborough NN8 24 A6
Goldsmith Dr NN17 6 D3
Goldsmith Rd NN8 29 E1
Goodens La NN29 35 H1
Goodhew Cl NN15 13 D6
Goodwin Cl NN8 24 A3
Goodwood Cl LE16 5 F5
Goodwood Rd NN10 33 G5
Gordon Rd NN8 24 B6
Gordon St, Kettering NN16 3 D4
Gordon St, Rothwell NN14 19 B2
Gordon St, Rushden NN10 32 D3
Gores La LE16 5 E6
Gorse Rd NN16 15 E4
Gorseholm Ct NN9 36 B4
Gosforth NN8 29 F1
Gotch Cl NN15 17 G5
Gotch Rd NN15 17 F5
Gough Dr NN15 17 F1
Goward St LE16 5 C5
Gower Cl NN15 16 C3
Grace Ct NN15 18 D3
Grafton Cl NN8 23 F4
Grafton Dr NN17 6 B4
Grafton Rd NN10 33 G3
Grafton St NN16 14 B4
Granary Ct NN10 27 F3
Granby Cl NN18 6 B6
Granby Ct NN29 35 F6
Grange Cl, Northampton NN6 34 B2
Grange Cl, Wellingborough NN29 31 H6
Grange Pl*, Judith Rd NN16 15 E4
Grange Rd, Broughton NN14 19 C4
Grange Rd, Kettering NN16 14 B5
Grange Rd, Stanion NN14 11 B5
Grange Rd, Stanwick NN9 20 C6
Grange Rd, Wellingborough NN9 23 G2
Grangeway NN10 32 D5
Grant Cl NN15 13 D6
Grant Rd NN8 24 B6
Grantham Walk NN18 8 C2
Grantown Cl NN15 17 E2
Granville St, Kettering NN16 3 D4
Granville St, Market Harborough LE16 5 C7
Grasmere Grn NN8 29 E1
Grasmere Rd NN16 14 A6
Grasmere Way NN10 27 F3
Gravely St NN10 32 D3
Gray Cl NN6 34 C3
Gray St NN29 31 G6
Grays Cl NN17 7 E4
Grays Dr NN14 11 B5
Greasley Walk*, Beanfield Av NN18 6 B6
Great Bowden Rd LE16 4 E4
Great Folds Rd NN18 8 A5
Great Park St NN8 24 A6
Green Cl NN8 23 F4
Green La, Burton Latimer NN14 18 B4
Green La, Great Bowden LE16 4 D2
Green La, Kettering NN16 3 C5
Green La, Market Harborough LE16 5 C7
Green La, Wellingborough NN9 20 C5
Green St NN29 35 G6
Greenacre Dr NN10 33 F5
Greenbank Av NN15 17 E1
Greenfield Av NN15 16 A1
Greenfield Way NN10 32 D4
Greenhill Rd NN15 16 A1
Greenhill Rise NN18 8 C2
Greening Rd NN14 19 A1
Greenland Walk NN18 8 B4
Greenlaw NN8 29 E1
Greenslade Cl NN15 16 B2
Greeve Cl NN18 8 C5
Gregory Walk NN18 9 E2
Greig Walk NN18 8 B4
Grendon Av NN17 6 B4
Grendon Rd NN6 34 A5
Grenville Cl, Corby NN17 6 A4
Grenville Cl, Kettering NN14 19 C2
Grenville Gdns LE16 5 B7
Gretton Brook Rd NN17 7 E1
Gretton Ct NN8 23 F4
Gretton Rd NN17 10 D1
Griffith St NN10 33 F4
Grimmer Walk NN9 26 B3
Grimsby Cl NN18 8 C2
Grindleford Cl NN14 12 A2
Grizedale Cl NN16 14 B2
Grombold Av NN9 21 F3
Grosvenor Cl NN15 17 G5
Grosvenor Rd NN15 17 G5
Grosvenor Way NN15 17 G4
Grove Pl NN9 21 F4
Grove Rd NN10 33 F3
Grove St, Raunds NN9 21 F4
Grove St, Rushden NN10 27 F5
Grove St, Wellingborough NN8 29 H1
Grove Way NN9 22 A3
Guillemot La NN8 24 A4
Gunnell Cl NN15 16 A2
Gunnsbrooke Cl LE16 4 E2
Gunthorpe Pl NN18 6 B6
H.E. Bates Way NN10 32 D3

Hachenburg Pl NN10 27 F6
Haddon Cl, Rushden NN10 33 E5
Haddon Cl, Wellingborough NN8 23 G3
Hadleigh Ho*, Rectory Ct NN10 33 E3
Hafod Cl NN18 8 D4
Hagley Cl LE16 5 F6
Haigh Dr NN15 17 F1
Halifax Sq NN18 8 C1
Hall Av NN10 33 E4
Hall Cl NN15 13 D6
Hall Dr NN9 22 B3
Hall La NN15 13 D5
Halls Cl NN17 10 D3
Hallwood Rd NN16 14 C4
Hamblin Ct NN10 33 E3
Hamilton Ct*, Elizabeth St NN17 7 E6
Hammond Way LE16 4 C4
Hampden Cres*, Windmill Av NN16 15 H5
Handcross Ct NN18 8 C2
Handcross Way NN10 33 F1
Hanover Cl NN15 17 G2
Harborough Rd, East Farndon LE16 5 A8
Harborough Rd, Great Oxendon LE16 5 D8
Harborough Rd, Kettering NN14 12 B1
Harborough Rd, Market Harborough LE16 4 A1
Harborough Rd, Rushden NN10 33 F4
Harborough Way NN10 33 G4
Harcourt Mews NN6 34 B3
Harcourt Sq NN6 34 B3
Harcourt St, Kettering NN16 14 D6
Harcourt St, Market Harborough LE16 5 B5
Harcourt St, Wellingborough NN9 21 G3
Harden Cl NN18 8 B6
Harding Cl NN15 17 F1
Hardwater Rd NN29 35 F2
Hardwick Cl NN8 23 H6
Hardwick Rd NN8 23 F5
Hargrave Ct NN9 36 A4
Harlech NN18 8 D3
Harpers Cl NN18 8 C6
Harrington Rd, Desborough NN14 12 A3
Harrington Rd, Rothwell NN14 19 A3
Harris Cl NN9 21 G2
Harris Rd NN17 6 B3
Harrison Cl, Market Harborough LE16 5 B8
Harrison Cl, Wellingborough NN8 23 G6
Harrod Rd LE16 5 D5
Harrogate Ct NN18 8 C1
Harrowden Rd, Finedon NN9 22 A3
Harrowden Rd, Wellingborough NN8 23 G3
Harrowick La NN6 34 A3
Hartland Dr LE16 5 E5
Hartley Dr NN15 17 G2
Hartwood Cft NN16 14 D1
Harvest Cl NN15 18 E3
Harvey Cl NN9 21 E4
Harvey Rd, Rushden NN10 33 E6
Harvey Rd, Wellingborough NN8 29 G2
Harwood Dr NN16 14 B2
Hastings Walk*, York Rd NN18 8 C1
Hatfield Cl NN8 23 E4
Hatton Av NN8 23 H6
Hatton Ct NN8 23 H6
Hatton Gdns NN8 23 H6
Hatton Park Rd NN8 23 H6
Hatton St NN8 23 H5
Havelock St, Desborough NN14 12 C2
Havelock St, Kettering NN16 14 C4
Havelock St, Wellingborough NN8 24 A6
Haweswater Rd NN16 13 C3
Hawkins Cl, Corby NN17 6 B3
Hawkins Cl, Kettering NN14 19 C2
Hawkshead NN8 29 E2
Hawson Cl NN15 16 C3
Hawthorn Cl NN15 18 D4
Hawthorn Rd, Burton Latimer NN15 18 D4
Hawthorn Rd, Kettering NN15 16 C2
Hawthorn Way NN8 23 G6
Hawthorne Rd NN9 22 C2
Hawthorne Walk*, Chestnut Av NN17 6 D3
Hay Cl, Corby NN18 8 C6
Hay Cl, Rushden NN10 33 F5
Hay La NN9 36 B5
Hayden Av NN9 22 C2
Hayden Rd NN10 33 F3
Hayden Walk NN10 33 G3
Haynes Rd NN16 15 E6
Hayway, Rushden NN10 32 D1
Hayway, Wellingborough NN9 36 A5
Hazel Rd NN15 16 D1
Hazelden Cl NN29 35 F6
Hazelwood La NN16 3 B5
Hazelwood Rd NN17 6 D5
Headingley Rd NN10 33 G3
Headlands, Desborough NN14 12 E2
Headlands, Kettering NN15 3 B6
Headway NN18 8 B6
Hearnden Ct NN8 29 G2
Hearth St LE16 5 B5
Heath Cote Gro NN14 12 A2
Heath Rise NN8 23 F5
Heath Way NN15 18 E1
Heather Ct NN10 33 E3
Heather Rd NN16 15 E3
Heatherbreea Gdns NN10 32 C2
Heathersage Cl NN14 12 A2
Heathfield Walk NN18 8 C2
Hecham Way NN10 27 F4
Helmsley Way NN18 8 C1
Hemery Way NN15 13 D6
Hemmingwell Lodge Way NN8 24 B4
Hemmingwell Rd NN8 24 A4
Hempland Cl NN18 8 B6
Henley Cl, Kettering NN15 17 F5
Henley Cl, Wellingborough NN8 23 F4
Henshaw Rd NN8 29 G3
Henson Cl NN16 13 D1
Henson Way NN16 13 C2
Hereford Cl NN14 12 E2
Herford Cl NN18 8 A4
Heritage Way, Corby NN17 7 G2
Heritage Way, Wellingborough NN9 21 H2
Heron Cl, Kettering NN15 18 B2
Heron Cl, Wellingborough NN8 24 A4
Heron Way NN8 24 B4
Herriotts La NN8 24 A6
Hertford Rd NN15 16 D4
Hesperus NN8 29 E1
Hever Cl NN10 33 G5
Heygate St LE16 5 C5
Hiawatha NN8 29 E1
Hickmire NN29 35 F4
Hidcote Cl NN8 29 F3
Hield Cl NN18 8 D5
High Hill Av NN14 19 B2
High St, Broughton NN14 19 B5
High St, Burton Latimer NN15 18 E3
High St, Corby NN17 7 G6
High St, Cottingham NN16 11 C1
High St, Desborough NN14 12 C3
High St, Earls Barton NN6 34 B3
High St, Finedon NN9 22 B2
High St, Great Doddington NN29 35 G1
High St, Higham Ferrers NN10 27 F6
High St, Irchester NN29 31 G5
High St, Irthlingborough NN9 36 A5
High St, Kettering NN16 3 B4
High St, Market Harborough LE16 5 C5
High St, Raunds NN9 21 G3
High St, Rothwell NN14 19 B2
High St, Rushden NN10 33 E2
High St, Stanion NN14 11 B6
High St, Stanwick NN9 20 C6
High St, Weldon NN17 10 E3
High St, Wellingborough NN8 23 H6
High St, Wollaston NN29 35 F5
High St South NN10 33 E4
High Street Pl NN8 30 A1
Higham Rd, Kettering NN15 18 E3
Higham Rd, Rushden NN10 33 E1
Higham Rd, Stanwick NN9 20 C6
Higham Rd, Wellingborough NN8 29 G5
Highbrook NN18 8 C2
Highcrest Av LE16 4 B4
Highcross St LE16 5 A5
Highfield Cres NN15 16 C4
Highfield Gro NN17 7 F4
Highfield Rd, Irthlingborough NN9 36 B4
Highfield Rd, Kettering NN15 16 C3
Highfield Rd, Northampton NN6 22 A6
Highfield Rd, Rushden NN10 32 C4
Highfield Rd, Wellingborough NN8 24 B6
Highfield St, Market Harborough LE16 5 B6
Highfield St, Wellingborough NN9 22 D2
Highgrove Ct NN10 33 F3
Hilda Pl NN16 15 F4
Hill Gdns LE16 5 A6
Hill House Gdns NN9 20 C6
Hill St, Kettering NN16 14 B5
Hill St, Raunds NN9 21 G3
Hill St, Wellingborough NN8 29 H1
Hillary Rd NN10 32 D4
Hillcrest Av, Burton Latimer NN15 18 D4
Hillcrest Av, Kettering NN15 16 D1
Hillside Av NN15 16 C2
Hillside Cres NN17 10 D3
Hillside Rd, Market Harborough LE16 5 D5
Hillside Rd, Wellingborough NN8 24 C4
Hillstone Ct NN9 20 C6
Hilltop Av, Barton Seagrave NN15 17 G5
Hilltop Av, Desborough NN14 12 B2
Hilltop Cl NN14 12 B2
Hind Stile NN10 27 F6
Hinton Av NN18 8 B2
Hinwick Cl NN15 16 D5
Hinwick Rd NN29 35 F6
Hobbs Hill*, Kettering Rd NN14 19 B2
Hockney Av NN15 17 G2
Hodge Way NN16 15 E5
Hogarth Cl NN8 23 H3
Hogarth Dr NN15 17 G2
Hogarth Walk NN18 9 F1
Holbush Way NN9 36 A3
Holcot Cl NN8 23 G3
Holdenby NN15 16 D5
Holdenby Cl LE16 5 F5
Hollands Dr NN15 18 E3
Hollington Rd NN9 21 G3
Hollowell Ct NN8 29 H1
Holly Cl LE16 4 C4
Holly Rd, Kettering NN16 14 D3
Holly Rd, Rushden NN10 32 B2
Holly Walk NN9 22 A2
Holme Cl NN9 23 G2
Holmes Av NN9 21 G4
Holmfield Dr NN9 21 H3
Holmfirth Walk NN18 8 C2
Holyoake Rd NN29 35 F5
Holyrood Walk NN18 8 D3
Home Cl, Corby NN18 8 C5
Home Cl, Wellingborough NN9 26 C3
Home Farm Cl NN18 8 C6
Home Farm Rd NN14 11 B5
Honiton Gdns NN18 9 F2
Hood Ct NN17 6 A4
Hood Walk NN15 17 E2
Hookhams Path NN29 35 G5
Hopper Walk NN18 9 E1
Hoppet Cl NN18 8 B6
Hopton Flds LE16 5 B8
Hornbeam Cl NN8 23 G6
Hornbeam Ct NN14 12 F3
Hornby Rd NN6 34 B2
Horrell Ct NN10 33 E3
Horrocks Way NN15 17 F1
Horse Mkt NN16 3 C4
Horsefair Cl LE16 5 B5
Horselease Cl NN18 8 B6
Horseshoe La LE16 4 E3
Horsham Walk NN18 8 C1
Hospital Hill*, Market Hill NN14 19 C2
Hove Rd NN10 33 G3
Hove St NN18 8 C1
Howard Av NN17 6 A5
Howard Ct NN8 24 B6
Howard Rd NN29 35 F6
Howard St NN16 3 A4
Howard Way LE16 5 B7
Howard's Ct NN29 35 F6
Howden Grn NN14 12 A2
Howe Cres NN17 6 A5
Hoylake NN8 23 F4
Hubble Rd NN17 7 F3
Hudson Cl NN18 8 C3
Hulme Way NN8 23 G4
Humber Gdns NN8 23 E5
Humber Walk NN17 6 C2
Hunt Cl NN8 23 H3
Hunt St NN18 9 E1
Hunters Rd NN17 10 C2
Huntingdon Gdns LE16 5 B7
Hurst Cl NN15 18 E1
Huxley Cl NN8 28 C1
Huxloe Pl NN16 3 B4
Hyacinth Way NN10 33 F6

Ibsen Walk NN18 8 B4
Imperial Ct NN10 33 E3
Inham Cl NN18 8 D4
Inwood Cl NN18 8 D4
Iona Rd NN17 6 C3
Irchester Rd, Rushden NN10 32 B4
Irchester Rd, Wellingborough NN29 35 G5
Ireton Rd LE16 5 B7
Ironstone Ct NN9 22 B2
Irthlingborough Rd, Finedon NN9 22 C2
Irthlingborough Rd, Wellingborough NN8 30 B2
Irving Gro NN17 7 E3
Ise Rd NN15 17 E1
Ise Vale Av NN14 12 E3
Ise View Rd NN14 12 D3
Isebrook Ct NN15 18 C3
Islay Walk*, Mull Dr NN17 6 B4
Ivy La NN9 22 B3
Ivy Rd NN16 15 E3
Ivydene Ter NN14 19 B5

Jacklin Ct NN8 23 F4
Jackson Cl LE16 5 C8
Jackson Way NN15 16 A2
Jacksons La NN8 23 H6
James Rd NN8 30 A3
James St NN29 31 H6
James Watts Av NN17 7 F3
Jasmine Ct NN16 14 D3
Jasmine Gdns NN10 33 E6
Jasmine Rd NN16 14 D3
Jean Rd NN16 15 E5
Jennings Cl NN10 27 E6
Jersey Cl NN8 24 B5
Jerwood Way LE16 5 D6
Joan Pyel Cl NN9 26 C3
Jobs Yd NN16 3 B4
John Clare Ct NN16 14 D2
John Clare Way*, Burns Dr NN17 6 C4
John Eagle Cl NN9 20 C5
John Gray Rd NN29 35 F1
John Lea Way NN8 30 A4
John Pyel Rd NN9 36 A5
John Smith Av NN14 19 D2
John St NN10 33 E3
Johnson Av NN8 30 A4
Jordan Cl LE16 5 E5
Jowett Cl NN15 17 G2
Jubilee Av NN18 3 A3
Jubilee Cres NN8 29 H3
Jubilee Ct NN9 22 C2
Jubilee Gdns LE16 4 D4
Jubilee St, Kettering NN14 19 B3
Jubilee St, Wellingborough NN9 36 A4
Jubilee Ter NN14 18 B4
Judith Rd NN16 15 E4
Jura Cl*, Shetland Way NN17 6 B3
Jutland Way NN16 3 A4

Kangaroo Spinney NN8 31 E2
Karlstad Cl NN18 8 B4
Kathleen Dr NN16 15 E4
Katrine Cl NN17 6 B3
Keating Cl NN15 17 H2
Keats Cl NN6 34 C4
Keats Dr NN16 14 D2
Keats Rd NN8 29 F1
Keats Way, Corby NN17 6 C4
Keats Way, Rushden NN10 32 C2
Keats Way, Warmonds Hill NN10 27 E6
Keebles Cl NN14 11 B6
Keld Cl NN18 9 E4
Kelmarsh Rd NN17 6 C5
Kelvin Gro NN17 7 F5
Kendal Cl, Rushden NN10 33 G4
Kendal Cl, Wellingborough NN8 23 F5
Kenilworth NN18 8 D3
Kenilworth Cl NN10 33 G4
Kenilworth Dr NN15 17 G2
Kenmore Dr NN14 12 D4
Kenmuir Rd NN9 22 B3
Kennet Cl NN8 23 E5
Kensington Cl NN10 32 C2
Kensington Gdns NN15 16 B1
Kensington Walk NN18 8 D3
Kent Cl NN17 6 B5
Kent Pl NN15 16 D4
Kent Rd, Rushden NN10 33 G2
Kent Rd, Wellingborough NN8 29 H4
Kenton Ct NN15 17 G2
Kerley Cl NN14 19 B6
Kestian Cl LE16 4 B4
Keston Way NN9 21 E4
Kestrel La NN8 24 A3
Keswick Dr NN10 33 G2
Kettering Parkway NN15 16 D5
Kettering Rd, Broughton NN14 19 C4
Kettering Rd, Burton Latimer NN15 17 H5
Kettering Rd, Isham NN14 18 A2
Kettering Rd, Market Harborough LE16 5 D6
Kettering Rd, Rothwell NN14 19 B2
Kettering Rd, Stanion NN14 11 B6
Kettering Rd, Weldon NN17 10 E4
Kettering Retail Pk NN15 16 C5
Kettering Venture Pk NN16 16 D5
Kettonby Gdns NN15 16 B2
Kielder Ct NN15 17 G5
Kilborn Cl NN8 23 H4
Kilborn Rd NN8 23 G5
Kilburn Pl NN10 33 E1
Kilby Cl NN8 29 G2
Kilnway NN8 23 F6
Kimbolton Rd NN10 27 F5
King St, Desborough NN14 12 D2
King St, Kettering NN16 14 C5
King St, Northampton NN6 34 B2
Kingfisher Way NN15 18 C2
Kings Av NN10 27 F4
Kings Ct NN14 12 D2
Kings Head Pl LE16 5 C5
Kings Meadow La NN10 27 E4
Kings Pl NN10 33 F3
Kings Rd, Market Harborough LE16 5 C5
Kings Rd, Rushden NN10 33 F3
Kings St NN8 24 A6
Kingsbrook NN18 8 C3
Kingsley Av NN16 14 B3
Kingsley Ct*, Kingsley Rd NN14 19 B1
Kingsley Dr NN17 6 C4
Kingsley Rd NN14 19 B1
Kingsmith Dr NN9 21 H3
Kingsthorpe Av NN17 6 B5
Kingston Way LE16 4 B3
Kingsway NN8 29 G2
Kingswood Pl NN18 8 B3
Kipling Rd, Corby NN17 6 C4
Kipling Rd, Kettering NN16 14 D3
Kipton Cl NN14 19 C2
Kipton Fld NN14 19 D2
Kirby Cl NN18 8 B3
Kirby Ct NN15 16 D5
Kirkwall Walk*, Stornaway Rd NN17 6 C3
Knapdale Cl NN16 14 B2
Knibb Pl NN15 17 G3
Knightlands Rd NN9 36 B3
Knights Cl, Corby NN18 8 B2
Knights Cl, Northampton NN6 34 B3
Knights Ct NN8 24 A6
Knights End Rd LE16 4 F3
Knoll St LE16 5 A5
Knowles Cl NN10 33 G2
Knox Ct NN8 30 B1
Knox Mews NN8 30 B1
Knox Rd NN8 30 B1
Knuston Dr NN10 32 C3
Kylesku Cres NN15 17 F2
Kynnesworth Gdns NN10 27 F4

Laburnum Cl NN8 23 G6
Laburnum Cres NN16 14 D4
Ladybower Cl NN16 13 C3
Ladywell Ct NN8 24 A4
Lake Av NN15 3 A6
Lakeside NN9 26 B3
Lammas Rd NN17 10 D1
Lamport Cl NN15 16 D5
Lancaster Cl NN29 35 F4
Lancaster Rd, Kettering NN16 14 D4
Lancaster Rd, Rothwell NN14 19 C2
Lancaster St NN10 27 F5
Lancaster Way NN10 33 G2
Lancum Ho NN8 23 G6
Landor NN8 29 F1
Landseer Cl NN8 23 H3
Landseer Ct NN18 9 E1
Langdale NN14 12 B2
Langdale Ct NN8 23 F6
Langdale Gro NN17 6 D4
Langham Rd NN9 21 F2
Langley Cres NN9 36 D1
Langley Ct NN15 18 D2
Langley Way NN15 16 C4
Langport Grn*, Glastonbury Rd NN18 6 A6
Langsett Cl NN16 13 C3
Langton Ct NN18 6 A6
Langton Pl NN14 18 A4
Langton Rd LE16 4 E1
Lansom Cl NN15 18 F1
Lapford Rd NN18 9 F2
Lapland Walk NN18 8 C4
Larch Cl NN29 31 F6
Larch Rd, Corby NN17 6 D3
Larch Rd, Kettering NN15 3 D6
Larchwood Cl NN8 23 G6
Larkhill NN10 33 E1
Larkin Gdns NN10 27 E6
Larkwood Cl NN16 14 C1
Larratt Rd NN17 10 D2
Lathkill St LE16 5 D7
Latimer Cl NN15 18 E3
Latimer Cres LE16 5 D6
Latimer Pk Ind Est NN15 17 H6
Latimer Rd NN17 6 D4
Launde Pk LE16 5 E6
Laurel Ct NN8 24 B6
Laurel Rd NN16 14 D4
Lavender Cl NN18 9 E4
Lavender Way NN10 33 F5
Lavendon Ct NN15 17 H5
Lavery Ct NN18 3 A3
Lawrence Cl NN15 17 H2
Lawrence Ct NN18 3 A3
Laws La NN9 22 B2
Lawson St, Kettering NN16 14 D5
Lawson St, Wellingborough NN9 21 G3
Lawton Rd NN10 33 F2
Laxton Cl*, Bute Cl NN17 6 B4
Laxton Ct NN15 17 H5
Laywood Cl NN9 21 F2
Laywood Way NN9 26 C3
Lea Way NN8 29 F1
Leah Cl NN18 8 B6
Leatherland Ct NN16 3 C4
Ledbury Rd NN15 17 F5
Lee Way NN9 21 F2
Lees St NN9 36 A5
Leeson Cres NN15 17 G3
Legion Cres NN16 13 D3
Leicester Cl NN16 14 B5
Leicester La LE16 4 A1
Leicester Rd LE16 4 A3
Leicester St NN16 14 B5
Leighton Cl NN8 23 H3
Leighton Pl NN8 30 A1
Leighton Rd NN18 3 A3
Lely Ct NN18 3 A3
Lenthall Sq LE16 5 C7
Lenton Cl NN14 19 B6

Leonardo Ct*, Leighton Rd NN18 9 E1
Lerwick Way*, Willow Brook Rd NN17 6 B4
Leven Way NN17 6 B3
Lewin Cl NN14 19 A2
Lewin Rd NN18 8 B6
Lewis Rd NN15 16 D3
Leyland Trading Est NN8 30 D1
Leyland Vw NN8 30 D1
Leys Av, Desborough NN14 12 E3
Leys Av, Rothwell NN14 19 B1
Leys Gdns NN8 24 C6
Leys Rd, Northampton NN6 34 A3
Leys Rd, Wellingborough NN8 24 B5
Lightfoot La NN16 11 B1
Lilac Ct NN8 23 G6
Lilac Gro NN10 33 F6
Lilac Pl NN15 16 D1
Lilford Pl NN16 15 E5
Lilley Ter NN9 36 B4
Lillington Ct NN18 6 A6
Lime Cl NN14 19 C6
Lime Ct NN9 36 B4
Lime Gdns NN9 36 C4
Lime Gro, Rushden NN10 33 E1
Lime Gro, Wellingborough NN8 24 A4
Lime Rd NN16 15 E4
Lime St, Rushden NN10 33 E1
Lime St, Wellingborough NN9 36 B4
Lime Ter NN9 36 B4
Lime Trees Gro NN17 7 F6
Lincoln Ct LE16 4 D4
Lincoln Walk NN18 8 C2
Linden Av, Rushden NN10 27 E4
Linden Av, Kettering NN15,16 14 D6
Linden Cl NN15 16 D1
Lindisfarne Dr NN15 17 G2
Lindisfarne Rd NN17 6 C3
Lindsay St NN16 14 C5
Lindsey Gdns LE16 5 B8
Lingfield Walk NN18 8 C3
Link Rd NN10 33 E6
Links Rd NN8 24 C3
Linley Dr NN14 12 B2
Linnell Way NN16 13 D1
Linnet Cl NN8 24 A4
Linnet Dr NN15 17 G4
Linnetts La NN10 27 F6
Lister Cl NN17 7 F3
Lister Rd NN8 24 A6
Litchfield Cl NN16 14 C2
Little Bowden Manor LE16 5 D6
Little La, Kettering NN14 11 C5
Little La, Wellingborough NN29 35 F4
Little Mdw NN18 8 B6
Little Park St NN8 24 A6
Little St NN10 33 F4
Little St*, Roman Way LE16 5 C5
Littledale NN8 23 F5
Littlewood St NN14 19 C1
Livingstone Cl NN14 19 D2
Llewellyn Walk NN18 9 E1
Lloyd Cl NN8 24 B3
Lloyds Rd NN17 7 G5
Loatland St NN14 12 B2
Lobelia Rd NN16 14 D4
Loddington Rd NN14 19 B3
Lodge Ct NN8 24 B6
Lodge Green Rd NN17 6 D5
Lodge Rd NN10 33 E6
Lodge Way NN9 26 B3
Logan St LE16 5 A5
Lomond Dr NN15 17 F1
London End, Northampton NN6 34 A3
London End, Wellingborough NN29 31 G6
London Rd, Kettering NN16 3 C5
London Rd, Raunds NN9 21 E1
London Rd, Wellingborough NN8 30 B1
London Rd, Wollaston NN29 35 E5
Long Acres Dr NN9 36 A3
Long Brimley Cl LE16 5 F5
Long Cl NN18 8 C5
Long Croft Rd NN14 11 A4
Longcroft Rd NN18 9 H2
Longfellow Dr NN16 14 D2
Longfellow Rd NN8 29 E1
Longleat Cl LE16 5 F6
Longleat Gro NN15 16 D5
Lonsborough Dr NN15 13 D6
Lonsdale Rd NN15 16 C3
Lorne Ct NN17 3 C2
Loseby Cl NN10 32 D5
Lotus Ct NN15 3 B6
Louisa Dr NN16 15 F4
Louth Dr NN10 33 G4
Lovap Way NN18 8 C5
Lovell Cl NN9 20 D5
Lovell Ct NN9 36 B4
Lower King St NN14 12 D3
Lower Pastures NN18 8 B6
Lower St, Desborough NN14 12 C3
Lower St, Kettering NN16 3 B4
Lower St, Wellingborough NN29 35 G1
Lower Steeping NN14 12 D4
Lowick Cl NN8 23 F4
Lowry Cl NN8 23 H3
Lubenham Hill LE16 5 A6
Lucas Cl NN9 26 C3
Lulworth Walk*, Glastonbury Rd NN18 6 A6
Lundy Av NN18 9 F2
Lupin Cl NN16 14 D3
Lydia Ct NN10 32 D3
Lyle Ct NN8 23 E4
Lynford Way NN10 32 D5
Lynmouth Pl NN18 9 F2
Lynton Gro NN18 9 F2
Lynwood Cl NN16 14 B2
Lytham Ct NN8 23 F4
Lyveden Pl NN16 15 E5
Lyveden Way NN18 8 D4

Macadam Rd NN17 7 F2
Mackenzie Rd NN9 21 F3
Mackworth Dr NN9 22 A2
Mackworth Grn NN9 22 B2
Madams Hill NN14 19 C1
Madeline Cl LE16 4 E3
Magellan Cl NN14 19 D2
Magnolia Dr NN10 33 F6
Maidford Rd NN17 6 B5
Main Rd, Northampton NN6 34 A2
Main Rd, Wilby NN8 28 D5
Main St, Kettering NN16 11 B1
Main St, Market Harborough LE16 4 D2
Malcolm Ct NN17 3 C1
Malham Ct NN8 23 F5
Mallard Cl, Northampton NN6 34 B1
Mallard Cl, Rushden NN10 27 F3
Mallard Dr NN15 18 C2
Mallery Cl NN10 33 G2
Mallows Dr NN9 21 F1
Malmo Cl NN18 8 B4
Malthouse Cl NN9 36 B4
Malton Walk*, Greenhill Rise NN18 8 C1
Malvern Cl, Kettering NN16 14 C1
Malvern Cl, Wellingborough NN8 29 G4
Manchester Rd NN29 35 F5
Manitoba Cl NN18 8 C3
Manning St NN10 33 F4
Manningham Rd NN9 20 D5
Mannings Rise NN10 33 F4
Mannock Rd NN8 29 G2
Manor Cl, Great Harrowden NN9 23 G1
Manor Cl, Irchester NN29 31 H5
Manor Cl, Kettering NN14 18 B4
Manor Ct, Kettering NN16 11 C1
Manor Ct, Rushden NN10 33 F5
Manor Ct, Wellingborough NN8 24 B6
Manor Dr, Corby NN18 8 B2
Manor Dr, Wellingborough NN9 36 C4
Manor Farm Rd NN9 21 G3
Manor Gdns NN9 20 D6
Manor House Cl NN6 34 B3
Manor House Gdns NN9 21 G2
Manor La NN6 34 B2
Manor Mews NN9 36 C4
Manor Pl NN15 16 C2
Manor Rd, Great Bowden LE16 4 E2
Manor Rd, Northampton NN6 34 B2
Manor Rd, Rothwell NN14 19 A2
Manor Rd, Rushden NN10 33 E6
Manor Rd, Stanion NN14 11 B5
Manor St NN9 21 G2
Manor Walk LE16 5 C6
Manor Way NN10 27 F6
Mansfield Cl NN14 12 C2
Mansfield St NN9 20 C5
Mantlefield Rd NN18 6 B6
Manton Ct NN10 33 F3
Manton Rd, Corby NN17 7 F2
Manton Rd, Rushden NN10 33 F4
Manton Rd, Wellingborough NN9 36 A4
Maple Dr NN8 23 G6
Maple Rd, Kettering NN16 15 E4
Maple Rd, Rushden NN10 33 G3
Maple Wood NN10 33 F6
Mapletoft St NN9 21 F4
Marcon Courtyard NN17 7 G3
Margaret Av NN8 29 H3
Margaret Rd NN16 15 E5
Marion Sq*, Dorothy Rd NN16 15 E4
Market Harborough By-Pass LE16 4 F1
Market Hill NN14 19 B2
Market Pl NN16 3 B5
Market Sq, Corby NN17 7 E6
Market Sq, Rushden NN10 27 F6
Market Sq, Wellingborough NN8 30 A1
Market St, Kettering NN16 3 B5
Market St, Wellingborough NN8 30 A1
Market Street Mews*, Market St NN16 3 B5
Markham Walk NN18 8 C1
Marks Cl NN9 20 D6
Marks Way*, Manor Dr NN18 8 B2
Marlborough Av NN8 23 G4
Marlborough Cl NN15 17 F1
Marlborough Way LE16 4 C4
Marlow Ho NN14 12 C3
Marriott Cl NN9 26 B2
Marsh La NN9 36 C4
Marshalls Ct NN9 21 F3
Marshalls Rd NN9 21 F2
Martha Wallis Ct*, Tanners La NN16 14 B5
Martin Cl NN10 33 E1
Martin Rd NN15 16 D3
Masefield Cl NN8 29 E1
Masefield Dr NN10 32 C3
Masefield Rd NN16 14 C3
Masefield Way NN17 6 C4
Matlock Way NN14 12 A2
Matson Cl NN14 19 A2
Matson Ct NN9 21 H2
Maunsell Rise NN14 19 A2
Maurice Rd LE16 5 B8
May Cl NN10 33 G6
Mayfield Rd NN14 12 E3
Maylan Rd NN17 7 F1
McGibbon Walk NN9 26 B3
McInnes Way NN9 21 F2
Meachem Cl NN14 19 B6
Mead Rd NN15 13 D6
Meadow Cl, Market Harborough LE16 4 D4
Meadow Cl, Rushden NN10 27 E5
Meadow Cl, Wellingborough NN8 24 D3
Meadow Dr NN10 27 E5
Meadow La NN9 20 C3
Meadow Rd, Kettering NN16 3 A5
Meadow Rd, Rothwell NN14 19 A2
Meadow St LE16 4 C4
Meadow Sweet Rd NN10 33 F6
Meadow Vw NN10 27 E4
Meadow Walk, Rushden NN10 27 E5
Meadow Walk, Wellingborough NN9 36 B4
Meadow Way NN9 36 B5
Meadway Cl NN15 17 E2
Mears Ashby Rd NN8 28 D4
Medina Rd NN17 6 C3
Medlicott Cl NN18 8 B6
Medway Cl LE16 5 E5
Medway Dr NN8 23 E5
Medwin NN8 29 E1
Meeting La, Burton Latimer NN15 18 E2
Meeting La, Corby NN17 7 G5
Meeting La, Kettering NN16 3 B4
Meeting La, Rothwell NN14 19 B2
Meeting La, Wellingborough NN9 36 B4
Meissen Av NN14 12 B3
Melloway Rd NN10 32 B3
Melrose Cl NN15 17 F2
Melton Rd NN8 24 C6
Melton Rd North NN8 24 B5
Melton St NN16 14 B4
Mendip Cl NN16 14 B2
Meon Cl NN17 6 C3
Merefields NN9 36 A3
Merestone Rd NN18 9 E3
Merri Vale Cl NN15 16 A2
Middle Grass NN9 36 A3
Middle St NN14 18 B4
Middledale Rd LE16 5 E6
Midland Bsns Units NN8 24 C5
Midland Rd, Higham Ferrers NN10 27 F6
Midland Rd, Raunds NN9 21 G2
Midland Rd, Rushden NN10 32 D2
Midland Rd, Wellingborough NN8 30 A1
Midland Works Bsns Centre NN8 24 C5
Milbury NN6 34 C4
Miles Cl NN9 21 E4
Mill Cl NN18 8 C5
Mill Dale Rd NN15 17 E1
Mill Est NN10 33 E6
Mill Flds NN10 27 F3
Mill Hill NN18 8 C6
Mill Hill Rd LE16 5 D5
Mill La, Kettering NN14 18 B4
Mill La, Northampton NN6 34 D3
Mill Rd, Cottingham NN16 11 C1
Mill Rd, Kettering NN16 3 D4
Mill Rd, Wellingborough NN8 24 B6
Mill Rd Ind Est NN8 24 C5
Millais Rd NN18 9 F1
Millard Cl NN8 29 F2
Milldale Gdns NN15 17 E2
Millennium Cl NN15 16 B3
Miller Cl NN15 16 D4
Miller Rd NN15 18 D3
Miller St NN9 21 G2
Millers Cl, Rushden NN10 32 D3
Millers Cl, Wellingborough NN9 22 C1
Millers La NN8 30 A5
Millers Pk NN8 30 A5
Millfield Av NN16 11 D1
Millholme Rd NN14 12 D4
Mills Cl NN6 34 B3
Milner Rd NN9 22 B2
Milton Av NN8 29 F2
Milton Ct NN16 14 D2
Milton Rd, Corby NN17 6 C4
Milton Rd, Wellingborough NN8 30 C4
Milton St NN10 27 F6
Minden Cl NN18 8 A5
Minehead Cl NN18 6 A6
Minerva Way NN8 23 F6
Minton Cl NN14 12 B3
Mirfield Cl NN18 8 C1
Mitchell Rd NN17 7 G2
Mitchell St NN16 14 C2
Moffatt Ter NN8 24 A6
Monks Rd NN29 35 F4
Monks Way NN8 30 A2
Monroe Cl LE16 4 B3
Montagu St NN16 14 C5
Montague St NN10 32 D3
Montcalm Cl NN15 17 F1
Montgomery Cl NN15 17 E1
Montrose Cl LE16 5 B7
Montrose St NN17 3 C1
Moonshine Gap NN9 22 A5
Moor Rd NN10 32 D2
Moore Cl, Corby NN17 6 C4
Moore Cl, Kettering NN15 17 G2
Moorfield Grn NN14 19 A2
Moorfield Rd NN14 19 A2
Moorhouse Way NN15 13 D6
Moorland Rd NN18 9 F1
Moorlands NN8 23 F4
Moreton Av NN8 29 F3
Moriston Cl NN17 6 C3
Morley St, Kettering NN16 14 C4
Morley St, Market Harborough LE16 5 A5
Morley Walk NN17 6 C4
Morris Av NN10 32 D4
Morris Cl NN8 22 D5
Mosel Cl NN8 30 A4
Motala Cl NN18 8 B4
Mount Pleasant NN6 34 B4
Mountbatten Way NN9 21 G3
Mountfield Rd NN9 36 B3
Muirfield Rd NN8 23 E4
Mulberry Cl NN8 23 G6
Mull Dr NN17 6 B4
Mulso Rd NN9 22 C2
Musson Cl NN9 36 A4
Myrtle Rd NN16 15 E3

Nansen Cl NN14 19 C2
Nansen Walk NN18 8 C4
Napier Cl NN8 28 D1
Narvik Rd NN18 8 B4
Nasbey Cl LE16 5 C7
Nasbey Sq LE16 5 C7
Naseby Cl NN8 23 G4
Naseby Rd, Corby NN17 6 C5
Naseby Rd, Kettering NN16 15 E5
Nash Ct NN15 17 G2
Nasmith Av NN17 7 F3
Neale Av NN16 14 B3
Neale Cl NN29 35 F4
Needham Rd NN9 20 C5
Nelson Dr NN14 19 D1
Nelson Rd NN17 6 A4
Nelson St, Kettering NN16 14 C4
Nelson St, Market Harborough LE16 5 B6
Nene Cl, Kettering NN15 17 G5
Nene Cl, Raunds NN9 21 G1
Nene Cl, Wellingborough NN8 23 E5
Nene Cres NN17 6 B3
Nene Ct NN8 30 D2
Nene Rd, Kettering NN15 18 C3
Nene Rd, Rushden NN10 27 E6
Nene Vw NN9 36 B4
Nepcote Cl NN15 17 E1
Nest Farm Cres NN8 24 A3
Nest Farm Rd NN8 24 A3
Nest Farm Way NN8 24 A4
Nest La NN8 24 B5
Netherfield Gro NN17 7 E4
Netherfield Rd NN15 16 D2
Neuville Way NN14 12 B3
Nevis Cl NN17 6 B3
New St, Desborough NN14 12 C2
New St, Irchester NN29 31 G5
New St, Irthlingborough NN9 36 B4
New St, Northampton NN6 34 C3
New St, Rothwell NN14 19 C1
New St, Wellingborough NN8 24 A6
Newark Dr NN18 6 B6
Newbridge La NN9 20 D6
Newbury Cl NN10 33 G2
Newcombe St LE16 5 C7
Newcomen Rd NN8 24 B6
Newham Cl NN14 19 B2
Newland St NN16 14 C5
Newman St, Burton Latimer NN15 18 D3
Newman St, Kettering NN16 3 C4
Newman St, Rushden NN10 27 F4
Newstead Ct NN15 16 D4
Newton Cl, Rushden NN10 33 G4
Newton Cl, Wellingborough NN8 22 D5
Newton Gro NN17 7 G3
Newton Rd, Higham Ferrers NN10 27 G5
Newton Rd, Kettering NN15 17 F5
Newton Rd, Rushden NN10 33 F3
Newton Rd, Wellingborough NN29 35 F5
Newtown Rd, Little Irchester NN8 30 C4
Newtown Rd, Raunds NN9 21 G4
Nicholas La NN9 36 B5
Nicholas Rd NN9 36 A5
Nicholas Way NN10 32 C2
Nichols St NN14 12 C2
Nichols Way NN9 21 F1
Nielson Rd NN8 24 C3
Nightingale La NN8 24 B3
Niort Way NN8 23 E5
Nippendale NN10 33 F3
Nithsdale Av LE16 5 C6
Nithsdale Cres LE16 5 D6
Nithsdale Rd NN17 6 D5
Noble Av NN9 36 C1
Norbury Cl LE16 5 B5
Norfolk Cl NN17 6 B5
Norman Way, Irchester NN29 32 A5
Norman Way, Wellingborough NN8 29 F3
Norris Cl NN15 17 G2
Norris Way NN10 32 C2
Norse Walk NN18 8 B4
North Av NN15 18 D2
North Cape Walk NN18 8 B4
North End NN10 27 F5
North Folds Rd NN18 8 A5
North Park Dr NN16 14 D3
North Rd NN6 34 B2
North St, Raunds NN9 21 G1
North St, Rushden NN10 33 E2
North St, Wellingborough NN8 24 A6
Northall St NN16 14 B5
Northampton Rd, Broughton NN14 19 B6
Northampton Rd, Kettering NN15 3 A6
Northampton Rd, Market Harborough LE16 5 C6
Northampton Rd, Northampton NN6 34 A2
Northampton Rd, Rushden NN10 32 A2
Northampton Rd, Wellingborough NN8 29 F3
Northbank LE16 5 C6
Northbrook NN18 8 C2
Northen Way NN8 23 H3
Northfield Av NN16 3 A4
Northfield Cl NN16 14 B3
Northfield Rd NN15 13 A5
Northleigh Gro LE16 5 A5
Northumberland Cl NN15 16 D4
Northumberland Rd NN15 16 D4
Norton Rd NN17 6 B4
Norton St NN14 19 C1
Norway Cl NN18 8 B3
Nunneley Walk LE16 4 D4
Nunnery Av NN14 19 A1
Nursery Dr NN8 24 B4
Nursery Gdns NN9 36 A4

Oak Cl, Irchester NN29 31 G6
Oak Cl, Kettering NN14 19 C5
Oak Cl, Market Harborough LE16 4 D4
Oak Cl, Wellingborough NN8 24 A4
Oak Rd NN15 14 D6
Oak St NN10 33 E1
Oak Ter NN9 36 B4
Oak Tree Cl NN14 12 C2
Oak Vw NN9 23 H2
Oak Way NN9 36 B4
Oakham Cl NN10 32 D5
Oaklands Pk LE16 5 D6
Oakleigh Cl NN9 21 F2
Oakley Dr NN8 29 G1
Oakley Hay Ind Est NN18 8 B5
Oakley Pond NN18 8 C6
Oakley Rd, Rushden NN10 32 D2
Oakley Rd, Corby NN17,18 3 C3
Oakley St NN16 14 B4
Oakpits Way NN10 33 G4
Oaks Dr NN10 27 E4
Oakway NN8 24 A4
Oathill Rise NN15 18 E2
Oban Cl NN15 17 F1
Obelisk Rd NN9 22 C2
Occupation Rd NN17 6 D5
Old School Mews LE16 5 B5
Oldenburg Rd NN18 8 A3
Oldland Rd NN18 9 E3
Oliver Cl NN10 33 F3
Ollerton Walk NN18 8 C1
Ollis Cl NN17 6 D4
Olympic Way, Kettering NN15 16 A3

Olympic Way, Wellingborough NN8 23 F6
Orchard Cl, Corby NN17 10 E3
Orchard Cl, Finedon NN9 22 B2
Orchard Cl, Rushden NN10 32 C2
Orchard Cl, Wollaston NN29 35 F5
Orchard Cres NN16 14 D4
Orchard Pl NN29 31 G6
Orchard Rd, Finedon NN9 22 B2
Orchard Rd, Raunds NN9 21 E4
Orchard St LE16 5 C5
Orchard Ter, Finedon NN9 22 B2
Orchard Ter, Wellingborough NN8 24 A6
Orient Way NN8 30 A1
Orion Way NN15 16 C5
Orkney Walk NN17 6 B4
Orlingbury Rd, Kettering NN14 18 A4
Orlingbury Rd, Wellingborough NN9 23 G1
Ormond Pl NN14 18 A4
Orton Pl NN8 23 F4
Orton Rd NN15 17 F5
Orwell Cl, Raunds NN9 21 F1
Orwell Cl, Wellingborough NN8 23 F5
Osborn Cl NN8 29 G2
Osborne Cl NN10 33 G1
Oslo Gdns NN18 8 A3
Osprey La NN8 24 B4
Ostlers Way NN15 16 B2
Oswald Rd NN10 33 G3
Oundle Rd NN17 10 F3
Ouse Cl NN8 23 E5
Outlaw La NN8 24 A6
Oval Cres NN10 33 G3
Oval Rd NN10 33 G4
Overdale Cl LE16 5 E6
Overfield Av LE16 4 D3
Ovett Cl NN15 16 A2
Owen Cl NN8 23 E6
Owen Mews NN8 23 E6
Owen Way NN10 27 E6
Oxford Cl NN6 34 C4
Oxford Rd NN17 6 C6
Oxford St, Finedon NN9 22 C2
Oxford St, Kettering NN16 14 B5
Oxford St, Rothwell NN14 19 C1
Oxford St, Rushden NN10 33 E6
Oxford St, Wellingborough NN8 29 H1

Packer Rd NN15 13 C6
Paddock Ct LE16 5 C5
Paddock La NN14 12 C3
Paddock Vw NN16 11 B1
Paddocks Rd NN10 32 C2
Pagent Ct NN15 16 B2
Pages Walk NN17 7 G6
Palk Rd NN8 30 B1
Palm Rd NN10 32 B2
Palmer Av NN9 36 D2
Palmer Cl NN8 23 F4
Palmer Ct NN8 23 H6
Paradise Av NN15 16 D3
Paradise La NN15 16 D3
Park Av, Kettering NN16 14 C4
Park Av, Rushden NN10 32 D4
Park Av, Wellingborough NN9 21 G4
Park Cl, Kettering NN14 18 B4
Park Cl, Northampton NN6 34 A3
Park Cres NN8 24 A6
Park Ct NN8 24 A6
Park Dr LE16 4 B4
Park Farm Ind Est NN8 22 D5
Park Farm Way NN8 28 D2
Park La NN6 34 A3
Park Mews NN8 24 A6
Park Pl NN10 33 F3
Park Rd, Burton Latimer NN15 18 D2
Park Rd, Irthlingborough NN9 36 B5
Park Rd, Kettering NN16 14 C3
Park Rd, Raunds NN9 21 G2
Park Rd, Rushden NN10 33 F3
Park Rd, Wellingborough NN8 24 A6
Park St, Northampton NN6 34 A3
Park St, Raunds NN9 21 G3
Park St, Wollaston NN29 35 G5
Park Vw, Kettering NN16 14 C4
Park Vw, Wellingborough NN8 30 B1
Parkers Ter NN9 22 B2
Parkham Ind Est NN10 32 B1
Parklands NN9 20 C5
Parsons Gro NN17 7 F3
Parsons Rd NN29 31 H6
Paterson Rd NN8 24 C2
Patrick Cl NN16 16 D4
Patrick Rd, Corby NN18 9 E2
Patrick Rd, Kettering NN15 16 D4
Patrick St LE16 5 C6
Paxford Cl NN8 29 G4
Peake Cl NN16 11 B1
Pear Tree Gdns LE16 5 B6
Pearmain Av NN8 24 A4
Pearson Mews NN29 35 F6
Peaselands NN14 12 B2
Pebble La*, Market St NN8 30 A1
Pebbleford Rd NN15 17 E2
Peck Way NN10 33 E2
Pegasus Ct NN15 16 D6
Pemberton St NN10 32 D3
Pembroke Cl NN10 33 F4
Pen Green La NN17 7 F4
Pendered Rd NN8 30 A4
Pendle Av NN16 14 B2
Pennine Way NN16 14 B2
Penrith Dr NN8 23 F5
Perkins Cl LE16 4 D4
Perkins Ct NN8 24 A6
Perkins Rd NN9 26 B3
Perry Cl NN15 16 B3
Perry La NN9 21 G2
Pershore Cl NN8 29 H5
Petworth Dr LE16 5 F6
Petworth Gdns NN18 8 C1
Pevensey Cl NN10 33 G4
Peveril Cl NN10 27 G5
Pevrel Pl NN14 12 A2
Philip Way NN10 27 G4
Phoenix Ct NN8 30 B2
Phoenix Parkway NN17 7 G1
Pightles Ter NN10 33 F4
Pightles Walk NN10 33 G4
Pigotts La NN15 18 E3
Pike Rd NN18 8 B5
Pilgrim Way NN8 29 H1
Pilot Rd NN17 7 H4
Pindar Rd NN8 29 H3
Pine Cl, Kettering NN14 12 E4
Pine Cl, Rushden NN10 33 E5
Pine Cl, Wellingborough NN29 31 G6
Pine Rd NN15 16 D1
Pinewood Cl NN16 14 C2
Pioneer Av, Burton Latimer NN15 18 D2
Pioneer Av, Desborough NN14 12 B4
Pipe La NN16 15 F3
Piper Cl NN8 23 H3
Pipers Cl, Kettering NN15 16 D1
Pipers Cl, Wellingborough NN9 36 B4
Pipers Hill Rd NN15 16 C1
Pipewell Rd NN14 12 D2
Pippin Cl, Rushden NN10 32 C2
Pippin Cl, Wellingborough NN8 29 H1
Pitt St NN8 29 G1
Playford Cl NN14 19 D2
Plough Cl NN14 19 B2
Plumpton Ct NN18 8 C1
Plumtree Av NN8 24 A4
Pochin Dr LE16 4 C3
Podmore Way NN14 19 B6
Polegate Ct NN18 8 C1
Pollard St NN16 14 B4
Polwell La NN15 17 F4
Ponder St NN14 19 C2
Ponds Cl NN9 21 G3
Pope Rd NN8 29 E2
Popham Cl NN9 21 F2
Poplar Cl, Rushden NN10 33 E5
Poplar Cl, Wellingborough NN29 31 G6
Poplar Pl, Wellingborough NN8 30 A1
Poplar Pl, Wollaston NN29 35 G6
Poplar Rd, Burton Latimer NN15 18 F1
Poplar Rd, Corby NN17 6 D3
Poplar Rd, Kettering NN16 14 D6
Poplar Rd, Wellingborough NN9 22 C1
Poplar St NN8 24 A6
Poplars Ct LE16 4 B4
Poplars Farm Rd NN15 17 H2
Poppy Cl NN10 33 F5
Portland Rd, Rushden NN10 33 F3
Portland Rd, Wellingborough NN9 36 B3
Portree Walk*, Willow Brook Rd NN17 6 C5
Post Office La LE16 5 D5
Potter Ct NN9 20 D5
Pound Cl NN18 8 C5
Pound Pl NN9 22 B2
Pratt Rd NN10 33 F3
Premier Way NN9 26 B3
Prentice Walk*, High St NN17 7 G6
Pressland Dr NN10 27 G5
Preston Ct NN15 18 E2
Pride Pl LE16 5 B7
Priestley Ct NN17 10 A1
Primrose Cl, Corby NN18 8 D4
Primrose Cl, Kettering NN16 14 D4
Primrose Gdns NN9 21 G3
Primrose Hill NN9 21 G3
Primrose Pl NN8 24 C6
Prince Rupert Av NN14 12 B3
Prince St NN6 34 B2
Princes Av NN14 12 D3
Princes St NN16 14 C5
Princess Way NN8 29 G3
Princewood Rd NN17 6 D2
Priors Cl NN10 32 C5
Priors Ct NN17 10 D2
Priors Haw Rd NN17 10 D2
Priory Rd, Wellingborough NN8 29 H2
Priory Rd, Wollaston NN29 35 F4
Prospect Av, Rushden NN10 33 E1
Prospect Av, Wellingborough NN29 31 F6
Prospect Cl NN29 35 F4
Purbeck Rd NN10 32 B3
Purvis Rd NN10 32 D3
Pytchley Ct*, Denford Rd NN17 6 B4
Pytchley La NN15 16 B6
Pytchley Lodge Rd NN15 16 C4
Pytchley Rd, Kettering NN15 16 D5
Pytchley Rd, Rushden NN10 32 D2
Pytchley Rise NN8 29 G2
Pywell Rd NN17 10 B1

Quantock Cl NN15 17 H5
Quebec Cl NN18 8 C3
Queen La NN8 30 A1
Queen St, Desborough NN14 12 D2
Queen St, Irthlingborough NN9 36 A4
Queen St, Kettering NN16 3 C5
Queen St, Market Harborough LE16 5 E7
Queen St, Northampton NN6 34 B2
Queen St, Rushden NN10 33 E3
Queen St, Wellingborough NN8 24 A6
Queens Rd NN29 35 F5
Queens Sq NN17 3 B3
Queensberry Rd NN15 3 B6
Queensway, Kettering NN15 18 C3
Queensway, Rushden NN10 27 F6
Queensway, Wellingborough NN8 23 F5
Quorn Cl, Kettering NN15 17 H4
Quorn Cl, Wellingborough NN8 29 F1
Quorn Rd NN10 32 D2

Racedown NN8 29 E2
Radnor Way NN15 17 G5
Raglan Cl NN10 33 G4
Ragsdale St NN14 19 C2
Railside Rd NN17 7 F6
Railway Ter NN16 14 B5
Rainsborough Gdns LE16 5 B7
Raleigh Cl, Corby NN17 6 A4
Raleigh Cl, Kettering NN14 19 D2
Ramsay Cl NN9 21 F2
Randsway NN9 21 G4
Ranelagh Rd NN8 24 B6
Rannoch Cl NN15 17 F2
Rannoch Way NN17 6 B3
Rathlin Cl*, Willow Brook Rd NN17 6 B4
Raunds Rd NN9 20 C5
Raven Dr NN15 17 G4
Ravensbank NN10 27 E6
Ravenscourt NN17 7 F4
Raymond Cl NN29 35 G6
Rectory Cl NN9 20 C5
Rectory Ct NN10 33 E3
Rectory La LE16 5 E6
Rectory Rd NN10 33 E2
Rectory Walk NN15 17 F3
Red Hill Cres NN29 35 F4
Redding Cl NN10 32 D6
Redgrave Cl NN15 16 A2
Redgrave Ct NN8 24 A3
Redhill Way NN9 23 G2
Redleich Cl*, Petworth Dr LE16 5 F6
Redwell Rd NN8 23 H5
Redwood Cl, Kettering NN14 12 E3
Redwood Cl, Wellingborough NN29 31 G6
Regal Ct NN10 33 G4
Regal Dr NN16 14 D1
Regency Ct NN9 22 C2
Regent Cl NN15 18 C2
Regent Rd NN15 18 C2
Regent St, Desborough NN14 12 D2
Regent St, Finedon NN9 22 B2
Regent St, Kettering NN16 14 C5
Regent St, Wellingborough NN8 24 A6
Reigate Walk NN18 8 C4
Rendelsham Cl NN16 14 B2
Reservoir Cl NN14 11 B5
Reservoir Rd NN16 14 C3
Restormel Cl NN10 33 G4
Reynolds Cl, Kettering NN15 17 G2
Reynolds Cl, Wellingborough NN8 23 H4
Reynolds Rd NN18 9 E3
Rhodes Cl LE16 5 A6
Ribble Cl NN8 23 F5
Ribblesdale Av NN17 7 E5
Richard Cl NN15 16 D4
Richardson Way NN9 21 G2
Richmond Av NN15 17 G2
Richmond Cl NN10 33 G4
Richmond Rd NN17 3 B1
Ridding Cl NN18 9 E3
Ridgeway NN8 23 H4
Ridgeway West LE16 4 C4
Ridgway Rd NN15 17 H1
Ridley St NN16 14 B4
Riggall Cl NN14 19 B6
Riley Rd NN16 13 D1
Ringstead Cl, Corby NN17 6 B4
Ringstead Cl, Kettering NN15 17 F5
Ringwell Cl NN9 36 A3
Ripley Cl LE16 5 F5
Ripley Rd NN16 11 D1
Ripley Walk NN18 8 C3
Risdene Ct NN10 33 E3
Ritchie Pk LE16 5 B8
Riverside LE16 4 E4
Riverside Ind Est LE16 4 F4
Rixon Rd NN8 24 B3
Roadins Cl NN15 16 B3
Roberts St, Rushden NN10 33 F3
Roberts St, Wellingborough NN8 29 G1
Robin Cl NN15 17 H4
Robin La NN8 24 B4
Robinson Cl NN16 13 D2
Robinson Rd NN10 33 F3
Robinson Way NN16 13 D2
Roche Way NN8 23 H5
Rochester Cl NN15 17 G2
Rochester Gdns LE16 5 B7
Rock Hill NN14 19 C2
Rock Rd NN9 22 C2
Rock St NN8 23 H6
Rockingham Ct NN10 33 E5
Rockingham Mews*, Stephenson Way NN17 7 F3
Rockingham Pads NN16 14 B2
Rockingham Rd, Corby NN17 6 B1
Rockingham Rd, Kettering NN16 14 B3
Rockingham Rd, Market Harborough LE16 5 E5
Rockleigh Cl NN9 22 C1
Rodney Dr NN17 6 B4
Roland Way NN10 27 E5
Rolleston Cl LE16 5 E6
Roman Cl NN17 10 E3
Roman Way, Irchester NN29 31 H6
Roman Way, Kettering NN14 12 C3
Roman Way, Market Harborough LE16 5 C5
Roman Way, Raunds NN9 21 H2
Roman Way, Rushden NN10 27 E4
Romney Rd NN18 3 A3
Rookwell Dr LE16 5 D7
Rose Av, Corby NN17 10 E3
Rose Av, Rushden NN10 32 D4
Rose Cl, Broughton NN14 19 C4
Rose Cl, Rothwell NN14 19 D2
Rose Ct NN29 31 H5
Rose Hill NN9 22 C2
Rosebery St, Burton Latimer NN15 18 D3
Rosebery St, Kettering NN16 14 D6
Rosedale Av NN17 3 A1
Rosemoor Cl LE16 5 F6
Rosemount Dr NN15 16 D3
Roses Cl NN29 35 F4
Rosewood Ct NN8 30 C2
Rosewood Pl NN16 14 D4
Rossendale Dr NN15 17 G5
Rossetti Rd NN18 3 B3
Rothwell Rd, Desborough NN14 12 C3
Rothwell Rd, Kettering NN16 14 A5
Rotten Row NN29 35 F5
Rotton Row NN9 21 G2
Roughton Cl NN15 16 C3
Roundhill Cl LE16 5 F6
Roundhill Rd NN15 16 C2
Rowan Av LE16 5 C7
Rowan Cl NN8 23 G6
Rowlett Cl NN10 27 F6
Rowlett Rd NN17 6 B4
Roxton Cl NN15 17 H5
Royal Ter NN16 14 C4
Royce Cl NN17 7 F3
Rubens Walk*, Turner Rd NN18 9 E1
Rufford Cl NN15 17 G4
Rufford Walk NN18 6 B6
Rugby Cl LE16 5 B6
Rupert Rd LE16 5 B7
Rushden Rd NN10 33 E6
Rushmere Way NN10 33 E1
Rushton Rd, Desborough NN14 12 D2
Rushton Rd, Rothwell NN14 19 C2
Ruskin Av NN8 29 E1
Russell Ct NN10 33 F3
Russell St NN16 3 C5
Russell Way NN10 27 E5
Russet Cl LE16 4 C4
Ruth Gdns NN16 15 E4
Rutherford Ct NN17 7 G3
Rutherford Dr NN8 22 D6
Rutherglen Rd NN17 7 E4
Rutland Cl NN17 6 B5
Rutland Ct NN14 12 B2
Rutland St NN16 14 D4
Rutland Walk LE16 4 D4
Rycroft Cl NN8 23 F6
Rydalside NN15 17 E1
Ryder Ct*, Saxon Way NN18 8 A
Ryder Vw NN8 23 F
Rye Cl NN10 33 F
Ryeburn Way NN8 23 H
Ryebury Hill NN8 25 E
Ryehill Cl, Kettering NN14 18 A
Ryehill Cl, Wellingborough NN9 26 C
Ryelands Cl LE16 5 F
Ryle Dr NN8 28 D

Sackville St, Kettering NN16 14 B
Sackville St, Wellingborough NN9 21 G
Saddlers Way NN9 21 E
Saffron Rd NN10 27 F
St Albans Cl NN15 17 G
St Albans Pl NN29 35 F
St Amandas Cl NN15 15 F
St Andrews Cl NN14 19 C
St Andrews Cres NN8 29 H
St Andrews Ct NN14 19 C
St Andrews St NN16 14 C
St Andrews Walk*, High St NN17 7 G
St Andrews Way NN14 19 C
St Annes Rd NN15 17 G
St Anthonys Rd NN15 17 G
St Augustines Cl NN15 17 G
St Barnabas Cl NN15 17 G
St Barnabas St NN8 29 H
St Bartholomews Cl NN15 15 G
St Botolphs Rd NN15 17 F
St Catherines Rd NN15 17 G1
St Cecilias Cl NN15 17 G1
St Chads Cl NN15 17 G1
St Christophers Cl NN15 17 G1
St Crispin Av NN8 29 H
St Crispin Rd NN6 34 C
St Crispin Way NN9 21 F1
St Davids Cl NN15 15 G
St David's Rd NN10 32 A1
St Dunstans Cl NN15 17 G
St Francis Cl NN15 17 G
St George's Way NN10 32 C
St Giles Cl, Barton Seagrave NN15 17 G
St Giles Cl, Desborough NN14 12 C
St James Cl NN15 17 G
St James Rd NN18 7 G
St James Rd Ind Est NN17 9 H1
St James' Cl NN10 33 F1
St Johns Pl NN17 7 G6
St Johns Rd NN15 17 F2
St Johns St NN8 24 A6
St Josephs Cl NN15 17 G1
St Katharine's Way NN29 31 G4
St Laurence Way NN9 20 C5
St Leonards Cl NN15 17 G1
St Lukes Cl NN15 17 G1
St Lukes Rd NN18 9 H1
St Magdalenes Rd NN15 15 F6
St Margarets Av NN10 32 D4
St Marks Cl NN15 17 G1
St Mark's Cl NN10 32 C3
St Marks Rd NN17 7 G6
St Marys Av NN9 22 B2
St Mary's Av NN10 33 E4
St Marys Ct LE16 5 D5
St Mary's Ct NN9 22 B2
St Marys Pad NN8 24 C6
St Marys Pl LE16 5 C5
St Marys Rd, Kettering NN15 3 C6
St Marys Rd, Market Harborough LE16 5 C5
St Marys Rd, Wellingborough NN29 35 G6
St Matthews Rd NN15 17 G1
St Michaels Gdns NN15 16 C2
St Michael's La NN29 35 F5
St Michaels Rd NN15 16 C2
St Nicholas Cl, Kettering NN15 15 F6
St Nicholas Cl, Market Harborough LE16 5 D6
St Nicholas Ct NN29 35 G1
St Nicholas Rd NN29 35 G1
St Nicholas Way LE16 5 D6
St Oswalds Cl NN15 17 G1
St Pauls Ct NN15 3 C6
St Peters Av NN16 3 C5
St Peter's Av NN10 32 C3
St Peters Cl NN14 11 C5
St Peters Ct NN9 21 G2
St Peters Way, Corby NN17 7 G6
St Peters Way, Wellingborough NN9 36 B4
St Philips Cl NN15 17 H1
St Rochus Dr NN8 30 A4
St Saviours Rd NN15 17 G1
St Simons Cl NN15 17 H1
St Stephens Rd NN15 17 G1
St Swithins Cl NN15 15 F6
St Theresas Cl NN15 17 G1
St Valentines Cl NN15 15 G6
St Vincents Av NN15 15 F6
Salcey Cl NN15 17 G5
Salem La NN8 24 A6
Salen Cl NN15 17 H5
Salisbury Rd NN8 24 C6
Salisbury St NN16 14 C4
Sallow Rd NN17 10 C1
Samuel Pl NN17 7 G4
Samuels Cl NN9 20 C6

Sandby Rd NN18 9 E2
Sanders Cl NN8 24 B2
Sanders Lodge Ind Est NN10 32 B2
Sanders Rd NN8 24 B2
Sanderson Cl NN15 16 A2
Sandpiper Cl NN15 18 C2
Sandpiper La NN8 24 B4
Sandringham Cl, Rushden NN10 33 E4
Sandringham Cl, Wellingborough NN8 29 G3
Sandringham Ct NN15 16 D5
Sandringham Way LE16 5 F6
Sandy Cl NN8 23 H5
Sapphire Cl NN16 14 D6
Sargent Rd NN18 9 E2
Sarrington Rd NN17 7 E4
Sartoris Rd NN10 32 D3
Sassoon Cl NN8 23 E5
Sassoon Mews NN8 23 E5
Saunders Cl NN16 3 B5
Saxby Cres NN8 30 C1
Saxilby Cl NN18 8 D2
Saxon Cl, Kettering NN14 12 C3
Saxon Cl, Market Harborough LE16 5 D5
Saxon Cl, Rushden NN10 27 E4
Saxon Ct NN18 8 A6
Saxon Dale NN16 14 C1
Saxon Rise, Northampton NN6 34 B4
Saxon Rise, Wellingborough NN29 31 H5
Saxon Way NN9 21 H3
Saxon Way East NN18 8 A6
Saxon Way West NN18 8 A5
Saxonlea Cl NN10 32 C2
Scapa Rd NN17 6 C4
Scarborough St NN9 36 A4
Scharpwell NN9 36 A3
School Hill, Kettering NN16 11 B2
School Hill, Wellingborough NN29 31 G5
School La, Cottingham NN16 11 C1
School La, Kettering NN16 3 C4
School La, Market Harborough LE16 5 C5
School La, Rothwell NN14 19 B2
School La, Rushden NN10 27 E4
School La, Wellingborough NN29 31 G5
School Pl NN18 8 D1
School Rd NN29 31 G5
School Walk NN8 30 A4
Scotland Rd LE16 5 D7
Scotland St NN16 14 D5
Scotsmere NN9 36 A3
Scott Av NN14 19 D1
Scott Cl LE16 4 C3
Scott Rd, Corby NN17 7 G6
Scott Rd, Kettering NN16 14 D3
Scott Rd, Wellingborough NN8 29 F2
Scotter Walk NN18 8 D2
Seagrave St NN15 16 C2
Seaton Cres NN18 9 F2
Second Av NN8 29 F2
Sedbergh Rd NN18 8 C2
Sedge Cl NN18 8 B6
Selby Cl LE16 5 C8
Selby Ct NN15 17 G2
Selby Walk*, Sedburgh Rd NN18 8 C2
Selsey Rd NN18 8 B1
Senwick Dr NN8 30 C1
Senwick Rd NN8 30 C1
Serve Cl NN8 30 A4
Settlers Flds NN15 16 B2
Severn Cl NN8 23 E5
Severn Ct NN15 18 D3
Severn Walk NN17 6 C3
Severn Way NN16 14 B3
Shackleton Cl NN14 19 D2
Shaftesbury Cl NN18 6 A6
Shaftesbury St NN16 3 D4
Shakespeare Dr NN15 18 C3
Shakespeare Rd, Kettering NN16 14 C3
Shakespeare Rd, Rushden NN10 32 C3
Shakespeare Rd, Wellingborough NN8 29 E2
Shakespeare Way NN17 6 D3
Shannon Cl NN10 33 G2
Shannon Way NN15 18 D3
Sharman Rd NN8 30 A1
Sharman Way NN14 19 D2
Sharwood Ter NN29 31 G5
Shaw Cl NN8 22 D5
Shearwater La NN8 24 B4
Sheep St, Kettering NN16 3 B5
Sheep St, Wellingborough NN8 30 A1
Sheffield Ct NN9 21 F4
Sheffield Walk*, Greenhill Rise NN18 8 C1
Sheffield Way NN6 34 B4
Sheila Pl NN16 15 F4
Shelley Dr, Corby NN17 6 D3
Shelley Dr, Rushden NN10 27 E6
Shelley Rd, Kettering NN16 14 C3
Shelley Rd, Wellingborough NN8 29 E1
Shelmerdine Rise NN9 21 G3
Shelton Ct NN29 35 F5
Shelton Rd, Corby NN17 10 B1
Shelton Rd, Wellingborough NN9 21 H4
Shepherds Hill NN29 35 H6
Shepton Ct NN18 6 A6
Sherborne Walk*, Glastonbury Rd NN18 6 A6
Sherrard Rd LE16 4 C4
Sherwood Cl NN17 6 D3
Sherwood Dr NN15 17 F5
Shetland Way NN17 6 B4
Shieling Ct NN18 8 A5
Shipton Way NN10 32 A2
Shire Rd NN17 6 B3
Shirley Rd NN10 33 E2
Shoemakers Ct NN10 33 E2
Shoreham Ct NN18 8 B1
Short La NN8 23 H6
Short Stocks NN10 33 G2
Shortwoods Cl NN9 21 G4
Shrewsbury Av LE16 5 F7
Shropshire Cl LE16 5 C5
Shropshire Pl LE16 5 C5
Shrubfield Gro NN17 7 E4
Shurville Cl NN6 34 B4
Sibley Rd NN9 22 D2
Sidegate La NN8 25 E2
Sidmouth Walk NN18 9 F1
Silver St, Broughton NN14 19 B4
Silver St, Kettering NN16 3 C4
Silver St, Wellingborough NN8 30 A1
Silverdale Gro NN10 32 B3
Silverwood Ct NN15 16 D2
Silverwood Rd NN15 16 D2
Simborough Way LE16 5 F5
Simpson Av NN10 27 F4
Sinclair Dr NN8 22 D4
Sir John Brown Ct*, Meadow Rd NN16 3 A5
Skagerrak Cl NN18 8 B4
Skegness Walk NN18 8 D2
Skinners Hill NN10 33 E3
Skippon Cl LE16 5 B6
Skipton Cl NN18 8 C2
Skye Rd NN17 6 B3
Slade Cres NN15 16 C3
Slade Valley Av NN14 19 D2
Slaters Cl NN10 33 G3
Slim Cl NN15 17 F1
Smith Ct NN9 21 F3
Smithfield Pl NN9 21 F3
Smyth Cl LE16 4 C3
Soane Cl NN8 24 A3
Soar Grn*, Shire Rd NN17 6 C3
Somerford Rd NN8 23 G5
Somerton Ct NN18 6 A6
Sondes Rd NN17 10 B1
Sorrell Cl NN14 18 A4
South Av NN15 18 D2
South Cl NN10 33 F4
South Folds Rd NN18 8 A5
South Pk NN10 33 F4
South Rd NN17 7 G6
South St, Kettering NN14 18 B4
South St, Wellingborough NN29 35 F5
Southall Rd NN17 7 G6
Southbrook NN18 8 C3
Southfield Dr NN15 17 G6
Southfields NN10 33 F4
Southgate Dr NN15 15 E6
Southlands NN15 16 C1
Southleigh Gro LE16 4 B4
Sovereigns Ct NN16 14 C1
Sower Leys Rd NN18 8 D2
Sparke Cl NN8 23 G4
Spencelayh Cl NN8 23 H4
Spencer Cl, Northampton NN6 34 C3
Spencer Cl, Wellingborough NN8 30 A4
Spencer Ct, Corby NN17 3 B2
Spencer Ct, Rushden NN10 33 E2
Spencer Par NN9 20 C6
Spencer Rd, Kettering NN14 11 B5
Spencer Rd, Rushden NN10 33 E1
Spencer Rd, Wellingborough NN9 36 A5
Spencer St, Burton Latimer NN15 18 D3
Spencer St, Kettering NN16 14 B4
Spencer St, Market Harborough LE16 5 B5
Spencer St, Rothwell NN14 19 C1
Spencer St, Wellingborough NN9 21 G3
Spencer Walk NN18 9 F1
Spey Cl NN8 23 F5
Spilsby Rd NN18 8 D2
Spinney Cl, Market Harborough LE16 5 A5
Spinney Cl, Rushden NN10 32 C3
Spinney Dr NN15 16 D3
Spinney Gro NN17 6 D5
Spinney La NN15 16 D3
Spinney Rd, Corby NN17 10 F4
Spinney Rd, Kettering NN15 18 E1
Spinney Rd, Rushden NN10 32 C4
Spinney Rd, Wellingborough NN9 36 B4
Spinney St NN9 21 F3
Spinney Ter NN9 36 B4
Spring Cl NN9 36 B4
Spring Gdns, Burton Latimer NN15 18 E2
Spring Gdns, Northampton NN6 34 B3
Spring Gdns, Rothwell NN14 19 C2
Spring Gdns, Rushden NN10 27 F5
Spring Gdns, Wellingborough NN8 29 H1
Spring Ho*, Wood St NN8 30 A1
Spring La*, The Swansgate Centre NN8 30 A1
Spring Rise NN15 16 C3
Spring St NN9 36 B4
Spring Ter NN9 36 B4
Springfield Cl NN15 16 C2
Springfield Gro NN17 7 F4
Springfield Rd, Kettering NN15 16 C2
Springfield Rd, Rushden NN10 33 G4
Springfield St LE16 5 D6
Spruce Ct NN16 14 D4
Spur Rd NN8 30 A4
Squire Cl NN18 8 B2
Squires Hill NN14 19 B2
Stablegate Way LE16 5 E6
Stadtpeine Cl NN17 6 B5
Staffa Walk*, Shetland Way NN17 6 B3
Stalbridge Walk*, Shaftesbury Cl NN18 6 A6
Stamford Cl LE16 5 C6
Stamford Rd NN17 10 D4
Stamford Rd NN17 10 E3
Stamford Rd, Kettering NN16 15 E5
Stamford Rd, Stanion NN14 11 A6
Stanier Cl NN16 14 A4
Stanier Rd NN17 7 F3
Stanion La NN18 7 H6
Stanley Mews NN8 24 B6
Stanley Rd NN8 24 B6
Stanley St NN14 19 C2
Stanton Cl NN8 24 B2
Stanway Cl LE16 5 E6
Stanwell Way NN8 29 F2
Stanwick Rd, Rushden NN10 27 F3
Stanwick Rd, Wellingborough NN9 21 E5
Station Rd, Burton Latimer NN15 18 A3
Station Rd, Corby NN17 7 F6
Station Rd, Desborough NN14 12 C3
Station Rd, Earls Barton NN6 34 B3
Station Rd, Finedon NN9 22 A1
Station Rd, Higham Ferrers NN10 27 F3
Station Rd, Irchester NN29 31 H5
Station Rd, Irthlingborough NN9 36 B4
Station Rd, Kettering NN15 3 B6
Station Rd, Market Harborough LE16 4 E3
Station Rd, Rushden NN10 33 E3
Stavanger Cl NN18 8 A4
Steel Rd NN17 7 H3
Steele Rd NN8 29 G1
Stephenson Way NN17 7 G5
Sterndale Cl NN14 12 A2
Stevens Ct NN6 34 B2
Stevens St LE16 5 B5
Stewarts Rd NN8 24 B2
Steyning Cl NN18 8 B1
Stinford Leys LE16 5 F5
Stockbridge Rd NN17 7 F3
Stockholm Cl NN18 8 B4
Stocks Hill NN9 22 A2
Stocks La NN17 7 G5
Stockwell Cl LE16 5 F5
Stockwood Dr NN17 7 F4
Stoke Rd NN14 12 B1
Stokes Rd NN18 9 E2
Stone Cl, Wellingborough NN8 24 A3
Stone Cl, Wollaston NN29 35 G6
Stonepit Dr NN16 11 D1
Stornoway Rd NN17 6 C3
Stour Rd NN17 6 C3
Stourton Cl NN8 29 G4
Stow Cl NN8 29 G4
Stratfield Way NN15 16 D5
Strathay Walk NN17 6 C3
Stratton Rd LE16 5 B8
Straws Cl NN9 36 A5
Stream Bank Cl NN8 29 F1
Streather Ct NN9 21 F4
Streather Dr NN17 7 E5
Streeton Way NN6 34 B2
Strode Rd NN8 24 B6
Stuart Cl NN16 3 D4
Stuart Rd, Corby NN17 3 B2
Stuart Rd, Market Harborough LE16 5 B6
Stubbing End NN18 8 C6
Stubbs Cl NN8 23 H4
Stubbs La NN15 17 H2
Studfall Av NN17 3 A1
Sturminster Way NN18 6 A6
Sturton Walk NN18 8 D2
Suffolk Pl NN15 16 D4
Sulgrave Dr NN17 6 B5
Sulleys Yd*, Roman Way LE16 5 C5
Summerfield Rd NN15 16 C2
Summerlee Rd NN9 22 B2
Summers Way LE16 5 B7
Sun Hill NN14 19 B2
Sunningdale Dr NN10 33 G5
Sunny Side NN6 34 A3
Surfleet Cl NN18 8 D2
Surrey Cl NN17 6 C6
Surrey Rd NN15 16 D4
Sussex Pl NN10 33 E1
Sussex Rd NN15 16 D4
Sutherlands Rd NN18 9 E2
Sutton Rd LE16 4 F2
Swale Cl NN17 6 C3
Swale Dr NN8 23 E5
Swallow Ct NN14 12 E2
Swallow Dr NN10 33 E1
Swan Cl NN15 18 C3
Swan Gdns NN18 8 D1
Swanage Ct NN18 6 A6
Swans La*, The Swansgate Centre NN8 30 A1
Swans Way NN10 27 F3
Swanspool Ct NN8 30 A1
Swanspool Par NN8 30 A2
Swinburne Cl NN16 14 D2
Swinburne Rd NN8 29 E1
Sycamore Cl, Corby NN17 7 E3
Sycamore Cl, Kettering NN16 15 E4
Sycamore Cl, Rushden NN10 33 F3
Sycamore Dr NN14 12 F3
Sydney St NN16 14 D6
Sykes Ct NN17 7 F4
Sylmond Gdns NN10 32 D5
Sylvanus Ho NN8 23 F6
Symington Way LE16 5 C5
Sywell Av NN8 23 F5
Sywell Rd NN8 22 B4
Sywell Way NN8 23 F5

Tainty Cl NN9 22 B2
Talbot Rd, Rushden NN10 32 D4
Talbot Rd, Wellingborough NN8 24 C6
Talbot Rd North NN8 24 C5
Talbot Yd LE16 5 C5
Tamar Grn*, Shire Rd NN17 6 D3
Tanfields Gro NN17 7 E4
Tann Rd NN9 22 B1
Tanners La NN16 14 B6
Tannery Cotts NN9 36 B5
Tasman Way NN14 19 C2
Taunton Av NN18 6 A5
Tavern Walk*, Tower Hill Rd NN18 8 B1
Tavistock Rd NN15 17 G5
Tavistock Sq NN18 9 F2
Tay Cl NN17 6 D3
Taylor Cl NN8 23 E4
Teal Cl, Kettering NN15 18 C3
Teal Cl, Rushden NN10 27 F3
Teal La NN8 24 B3
Teasel Cl NN10 33 F6
Tebbutt's Yd NN6 34 B3
Tees Cl NN8 23 F5
Teesdale Rd NN17 6 D5
Telford Way NN16 13 D2
Telford Way Ind Est NN16 13 D1
Telfords La NN17 7 F4
Templar Rd NN15 17 F1
Tenbury Way NN14 19 D1
Tennyson Dr NN17 6 C3
Tennyson Rd, Kettering NN16 3 C5
Tennyson Rd, Rothwell NN14 19 A1
Tennyson Rd, Rushden NN10 32 C3
Tennyson Rd, Wellingborough NN8 29 F2
Tenter Cl NN10 27 F6
Tenter La NN9 22 B2
Tentsmuir Cl NN16 14 B2
Tettenhall Cl NN18 8 B5
Teviot Cl NN17 6 C3
Tewkesbury Cl NN8 23 F4
Tewkesbury Dr NN10 33 G5
Thames Ct NN15 18 D3
Thames Rd NN8 23 F4
Thames Rise NN16 14 B3
Thames Walk NN17 6 D3
Thatch Meadow Dr LE16 5 F5
Thatchers Gdns NN15 18 E2
The Avenue, Kettering NN14 19 C1
The Avenue, Stanwick NN9 20 D6
The Avenue, Wellingborough NN8 24 A5
The Banks NN9 23 H2
The Barns NN29 31 H4
The Broadway LE16 4 C4
The Brontes NN17 6 C3
The Cloisters NN8 30 B2
The Close, Kettering NN15 16 C2
The Close, Wellingborough NN9 36 B5
The Cottons NN8 23 F4
The Crescent, Burton Latimer NN15 18 E1
The Crescent, Kettering NN15 16 B1
The Crescent, Market Harborough LE16 4 D4
The Crescent, Rothwell NN14 19 B2
The Crescent, Rushden NN10 32 C3
The Dale NN8 23 E6
The Dell NN6 34 B3
The Delves NN9 21 F3
The Downs NN9 23 G2
The Drive, Kettering NN15 3 B6
The Drive, Rushden NN10 33 F4
The Drive, Wellingborough NN8 30 A2
The Embankment NN8 30 C3
The Fairway, Kettering NN15 16 B2
The Fairway, Wellingborough NN9 23 G2
The Flatlets NN9 36 B4
The Furlongs LE16 5 F5
The Gables NN15 3 B6
The Gap NN29 35 G5
The Gardens, Cottingham NN16 11 A3
The Gardens, Kettering NN16 14 B4
The Glade NN9 23 H2
The Green LE16 4 E2
The Grove, Corby NN18 7 H6
The Grove, Kettering NN15 3 C6
The Grove, Wellingborough NN29 35 F6
The Hawthorns, Kettering NN14 12 E3
The Hawthorns, Rushden NN10 27 F5
The Headlands, Market Harborough LE16 4 D4
The Headlands, Wellingborough NN8 23 H4
The Heathers NN29 35 G5
The Hedges NN10 33 F1
The Heights LE16 5 F6
The Hill NN16 11 B2
The Hollies, Rushden NN10 27 E6
The Hollies, Wellingborough NN8 23 G6
The Jamb NN17 7 G5
The John White Cl NN10 27 F5
The Lawns NN18 8 B2
The Lilly Homes NN8 30 A2
The Maltings, Kettering NN14 19 B2
The Maltings, Wellingborough NN29 35 F4
The Market Sq NN17 3 B2
The Meadows NN9 23 G2
The Mill Glade NN14 18 B4
The Nook, Corby NN17 7 G6
The Nook, Kettering NN16 11 D1
The Octagon NN17 7 G4
The Old Stables NN29 31 H4
The Old Vineyard NN10 27 F5
The Osiers NN14 12 F3
The Oval, Corby NN17 10 F3
The Oval, Market Harborough LE16 4 C4
The Paddock NN9 21 E5
The Pastures, Market Harborough LE16 5 A5
The Pastures, Wellingborough NN9 23 H2
The Poplars*, Poplars Ct LE16 4 B4
The Promenade NN8 23 H6
The Pyghtle, Northampton NN6 34 B2
The Pyghtle, Wellingborough NN8 23 H4
The Pyghtles NN29 35 F6
The Ridge NN29 35 H1
The Ridgeway LE16 4 D4
The Ridings NN14 12 A2
The Rylstone NN8 28 D1
The Saplings NN16 14 C1
The Shortlands NN9 36 D1
The Sidings NN9 26 B3
The Slips NN9 23 G1
The Smithy NN10 33 E4
The Sorrells NN14 18 B3
The Square, Market Harborough LE16 5 C6
The Square, Northampton NN6 34 B3
The Square, Wellingborough NN9 21 G3
The Swansgate Centre NN8 30 A1
The Wells NN9 22 B2
The Woodlands LE16 4 A4
The Wroe NN10 27 F4
Thetford Cl NN18 8 B5
Third Av NN8 29 F2
Thirlmere NN8 23 F6
Thirlmere Cl NN16 13 D3
Thirsk Rd NN18 8 D1
Thoday Cl NN14 19 B6
Thomas Cl NN18 9 E2
Thomas Flawn Rd NN9 26 B3
Thomas Rd NN15 16 D3
Thomas St NN8 24 B6
Thompson Way NN15 16 A2
Thorn Cl NN16 14 C2
Thornborough Cl LE16 5 E6
Thornbridge Cl NN10 32 D4
Thorne Ct NN18 8 D1

Thorngate St NN16	3 D4		Upperfield Gro NN17	7 E4		Watson Cl NN8	23 E4		Westminster Dr NN15	17 G2		Windsor Ct LE16	4 B
Thoroughsale Rd NN17	6 D4		Uppingham Rd NN18	6 A6		Wavell Cl NN15	17 F1		Westminster Rd NN8	23 G4		Windsor Gdns NN16	14 B
Thorpe Cl NN8	23 E6					Waver Cl NN18	9 E3		Westminster Walk*,			Windsor Pl NN17	3 B
Thorpe Rd NN6	34 B5		Vale St NN16	14 B4		Waverley Av NN17	7 G6		Dunedin Rd NN8	8 D3		Windsor Rd,	
Thorpe St NN9	21 G3		Valley Rd NN8	29 H3		Waverley Rd NN15	16 D2		Westmorland Dr NN14	12 E2		Rushden NN10	33 F
Thrapston Rd NN14	22 C2		Valley Rise NN14	12 D4		Weaver Cl NN16	8 B6		Weston Walk NN18	8 B6		Windsor Rd,	
Thrift St, Irchester NN29	31 G5		Valley Walk NN16	15 E6		Weavers Rd NN8	29 G1		Westover Rd NN15	13 D4		Wellingborough NN8	29 H
Thrift St, Rushden NN10	27 E6		Valley Way LE16	5 F5		Webb Rd NN9	21 F2		Westville Cotts NN8	29 H1		Wingate Cl NN15	17 F
Thrift St, Wollaston NN29	35 F5		Vancouver Cl NN18	8 C4		Webster Cl NN9	21 G2		Westwood Walk NN18	6 C6		Winstanley Rd NN8	30 B
Thrush La NN8	24 B4		Vara Cl NN8	8 B4		Wedgwood Cl NN14	12 B3		Wetenhall Rd NN9	20 D5		Winterbourne Ct NN16	6 A
Thurburn Cl NN14	19 C4		Vardon Cl NN8	23 F4		Wedmore Ct NN18	6 A6		Weymouth Cl NN18	6 A6		Winthorpe Walk NN18	6 B
Thurlow Rd NN8	6 C3		Vauxley Cl NN8	23 H3		Weekley Glebe Rd NN16	14 D3		Wharf Rd NN10	27 E5		Wisteria Cl NN10	33 E
Thurston Dr NN15	16 A2		Vaughan Cl LE16	5 C8		Weekley Wood La NN16	14 C1		Wharfedale Rd NN17	7 E3		Woburn Cl NN16	3 E
Timpson Cl NN16	14 C3		Vaux Rd NN8	24 A1		Weir Cl NN8	23 H4		Wharton Cl NN18	6 A6		Woburn Cl NN15	33 E
Timson Cl LE16	4 B3		Venture Cl NN17	10 D2		Welbeck Cl, Corby NN18	8 C1		Wheatcroft Gdns NN10	33 F3		Wold Rd NN15	18 F
Tingdene Rd NN9	22 B2		Vian Way NN17	6 B4		Welbeck Ct,			Wheatfield Dr NN15	18 E3		Wolfe Cl NN15	17 F
Tintagel Cl NN10	33 G4		Vicarage Cl NN8	23 G5		Kettering NN15	17 F2		Wheatley Av NN17	3 C1		Wollaston Rd NN29	31 H
Tintern Ct NN15	17 G2		Vicarage Farm Rd NN8	23 G5		Welbourne Cl NN9	21 F2		Wheelwright Cl NN9	21 H2		Wood St, Corby NN17	3 A
Tithe Barn Cl NN9	21 G2		Viceroy Cl NN9	21 H3		Weldon Cl NN8	23 G4		Wheelwright Ho*,			Wood St, Kettering NN16	14 C
Tithe Barn Rd NN8	30 A1		Vickers Cl NN14	19 D2		**Weldon North**			High St NN14	19 B2		Wood St, Rushden NN10	27 F
Titley Bawk Av NN6	34 C1		Victoria Av LE16	4 B4		**Ind Est NN17**	**10 D1**		Wherside NN8	23 H4		Wood St,	
Titty Ho NN9	21 F4		Victoria Cl,			Weldon Rd NN17	7 G6		Whiston Dene NN8	23 H4		Wellingborough NN8	29 H
Todmorden Cl NN18	8 C1		Northampton NN6	34 B2		**Weldon South**			White House Ct NN10	33 F4		Woodbreach Dr LE16	5 B
Tollbar NN10	27 F6		Victoria Cl, Rushden NN10	33 F2		**Ind Est NN17**	**10 B4**		**White House**			Woodcock St NN15	18 F
Toller Pl NN15	17 F4		Victoria Ct,			Weldon St*,			**Ind Est NN6**	**34 A1**		Woodfield Gro NN17	7 E
Tollgate Rd NN18	7 H6		Kettering NN16	19 B1		Catesby St NN16	14 D5		White Post Ct NN17	14 D5		Woodford Cl NN15	17 F
Top Farm La NN29	35 H1		Victoria Ct,			Welford Av NN9	36 D1		White Way NN16	34 A2		Woodgate Cl LE16	5 F
Tordoff Pl NN16	3 C4		Rushden NN10	33 E2		Welford Gro NN17	6 A6		Whitefield Way NN9	21 F2		Woodland Av NN15	17 G
Torksey Cl NN18	8 B5		Victoria Rd, Finedon NN9	22 B2		Welham Rd LE16	4 E2		Whiteford Dr NN15	16 C3		Wood St NN16	14 C
Torridge Cl NN16	13 D1		Victoria Rd,			Well La NN14	19 C2		Whitefriars NN18	32 C4		Woodland Dr NN15	18 E
Torridon Cl NN17	6 C3		Rushden NN10	33 E2		Well St NN9	22 B2		Whitehills Rd NN14	12 A2		Woodland Rd NN10	32 D
Torrington Cres NN8	23 G5		**Victoria**			**Welland Bsns Pk**			Whiteman St NN14	19 B2		Woodlands Av NN17	7 E
Torrington Grn NN8	23 G5		**Retail Pk NN8**	**30 B3**		**LE16**	**5 E5**		Whites Rise NN9	36 A5		Woodlands Grange NN6	34 C
Torrington Rd NN8	23 G5		Victoria St,			Welland Cl NN9	21 F1		Whitney Cl NN15	17 G2		Woodlands La NN18	8 C
Torrington Way NN8	23 G5		Burton Latimer NN15	18 D2		Welland Ct,			Whitney Rd NN15	18 D3		Woodlands Rd,	
Torvill Cres NN15	16 A2		Victoria St,			Burton Latimer NN15	18 D2		Whitsundale Cl NN9	22 B2		Corby NN17	10 F
Totnes Cl NN18	9 F2		Desborough NN14	12 C3		Welland Ct,			Whittam Cl NN8	21 F1		Woodlands Rd,	
Tower Cl NN9	22 D2		Victoria St, Kettering NN16	3 C4		Desborough NN14	12 C2		Whittemore Rd NN10	33 G2		Wellingborough NN29	31 F
Tower Ct NN29	35 H5		Victoria St,			Welland Park Rd LE16	5 B6		Whittle Cl NN8	23 E5		Woodnewton Way NN17	6 C
Tower Hill Rd NN18	8 B5		Northampton NN6	34 B2		Welland Rd NN16	14 B3		Whittle Rd NN17	7 H4		Woods Cl NN18	33 E
Townley Way NN6	34 A2		Victoria St,			Welland Vale Rd NN17	6 D3		Whitworth Av NN17	7 G3		Woodstock Cl NN8	23 G
Townsend Cl NN8	29 H1		Wellingborough NN9	36 A5		Welland View Rd NN16	11 D1		Whitworth Rd NN8	34 B3		Woodwell Hill NN14	12 B
Townsend Leys NN10	27 F3		Viking Cl NN16	14 D2		Wellingborough Rd,			Whitworth Cres NN6	24 C6		Worcester Dr LE16	4 C
Townwell La NN29	31 H5		Viking Way NN18	8 A4		Broughton NN14	19 B6		Whitworth Way NN9	23 H5		Wordsworth Av NN17	4 C
Trafalgar Rd NN16	3 A4		Villa La NN9	20 C6		Wellingborough Rd,			Whytewell Rd NN8	23 H5		Wordsworth Rd,	
Trafford Rd NN10	33 G3		Villa Rise NN10	27 E4		Burrow's Bush NN8	25 E3		Wick Cl NN18	9 E3		Kettering NN16	14 C
Trefoil Cl NN10	33 F6		Vine Hill Cl NN10	27 E4		Wellingborough Rd,			Wicksteed Cl NN15	16 D4		Wordsworth Rd,	
Trent Cl NN8	23 F5		Vine Hill Dr NN10	27 E5		Finedon NN9	22 B3		Wilby Cl NN17	6 B4		Wellingborough NN8	28 D
Trent Cres NN15	18 D3		Violet Cl NN18	9 E4		Wellingborough Rd,			Wilby La NN9	35 G1		Worksop Gdns*,	
Trent Rd, Corby NN17	6 D3		Vivian Rd NN8	24 C6		Great Harrowden NN9	23 G1		Wilby Rd NN6	28 A3		Mantlefield Rd NN18	6 B
Trent Rd, Kettering NN16	14 C5		Wadcroft*, High St NN16	3 B4		Wellingborough Rd,			Wilby Way NN8	29 F3		Worthing Rd NN18	8 C
Tresham St,			Wake Cl NN8	30 A4		Irthlingborough NN9	25 H4		Wilbye Grange NN8	29 F3		Wren Cl NN15	17 H
Kettering NN16	14 C5		Wakefield Cl NN18	29 E1		Wellingborough Rd,			Wilce Av NN8	30 A4		Wroe Cl NN18	8 B
Tresham St,			Walcot Rd LE16	5 C8		Isham NN14	18 B4		Wildacre Rd NN10	32 B3		Wyatt St NN16	3 D
Rothwell NN14	19 C2		Wales Cl*, Wales St NN14	19 B2		Wellingborough Rd,			Wilkie Cl NN15	13 D6		Wyckley Cl NN9	36 A
Trevithick Rd NN17	7 H3		Wales St NN14	19 B2		Northampton NN6	34 B1		Willetts Cl NN17	7 E6		Wye Cl NN8	23 E
Trimble Cl NN18	8 D3		Walker Sq NN8	23 F4		Wellingborough Rd,			William St,			Wykeham Rd NN10	27 F
Trinity Centre NN8	**22 D4**		Walkers Way NN9	22 B2		Rushden NN10	32 B2		Burton Latimer NN15	18 D2		Wymington Pk NN10	33 F
Trinity Cl NN14	19 A2		Wallis Cl NN18	28 D1		Wellington Rd NN8	21 F4		William St,			Wymington Rd NN10	33 E
Trinity Rd NN14	19 A2		Wallis Cres NN15	16 D1		Wellington St NN16	14 C4		Kettering NN16	14 C4		Wyndham Way NN18	13 C
Trinity Walk*,			Wallis Rd NN15	16 D2		Wells Cl NN15	13 D6		William St,			Wyre Pl NN16	14 B
Oakley Rd NN18	9 E2		Walmer Cl NN10	33 G4		Wells Gro NN18	6 B6		Wellingborough NN9	22 C2		Yardley Cl NN17	6 D
Tromso Cl NN18	8 B4		Walnut Cl NN17	10 E3		Wensleydale Pk NN16	7 C4		William Steele Way NN18	27 F5		Yarrow Cl NN8	29 E
Troon Cres NN8	23 E4		Walnut Cres NN16	14 D4		Wentin Cl NN18	8 D5		William Trigg Cl NN15	26 C3		Yarrow Cl NN10	32 B
Tudor Ct*,			Walsingham Av NN15	17 F2		Wentworth Av NN16	23 E4		Williams Way NN10	27 E6		Yarwell Ct NN15	16 C
Victoria St NN16	14 C5		Waltham Cl NN17	6 D3		Wentworth Rd,			Willow's Way NN29	35 G6		Yateley Dr NN16	17 H
Tudor Walk NN10	33 F2		Walton Cl NN18	8 B4		Rushden NN16	33 E3		Willow Brook Rd NN17	6 B4		Yeadon Cl NN10	32 C
Tudor Way NN8	23 G4		Wansell Rd NN15	10 C2		Wentworth Rd,			Willow Cl NN14	12 E3		Yeldon Ct NN18	24 B
Tulip Dr NN10	33 F6		Wansford Pl NN17	6 B4		Wellingborough NN9	22 D1		Willow Cres LE16	5 A6		Yeoman Ct*,	
Tunwell La NN17	7 G5		Wantage Cl NN10	33 G5		Wesley Cl NN9	21 G3		Willow Herb Cl NN10	33 F6		Meeting La NN15	18 E
Turnberry Ct NN8	23 E4		Wantage Pl NN29	31 H5		Wessex Cl NN16	14 B2		Willow La NN14	11 B6		Yeomanry Cl LE16	5 C
Turnbrook Cl NN9	36 A3		Wantage Rd NN29	31 H5		West Av NN15	18 D2		Willow Rd NN15	13 D5		Yew Cl NN17	7 C
Turnells Mill La NN8	30 A4		Wardle Ct*,			West Cres NN10	32 D2		**Willowbrook East**			Yew Tree Cl NN16	16 D
Turner Cl NN15	17 G2		Crown St NN16	14 C5		West Furlong NN15	13 D5		**Ind Est NN17**	**10 A1**		York Cl NN10	27 F
Turner Rd, Corby NN17	3 A3		Wareham Grn*,			West Glebe Rd NN17	7 E4		Wilmington Walk*,			York Rd,	
Turner Rd,			Warkton La NN15	6 B6		West St, Broughton NN14	19 B5		Farmstead Rd NN18	9 E2		Higham Ferrers NN10	27 F
Wellingborough NN8	23 H3		Warkton La NN15	17 H2		West St, Kettering NN16	3 B5		Wilson Cl LE16	5 E5		York Rd, Rushden NN10	33 F
Turnpike Cl LE16	4 B4		Warkton Rd NN17	17 H3		West St,			Wilson Cres NN9	36 B5		York Rd,	
Tweed Cl NN15	18 B4		Warkton Way NN17	6 B4		Northampton NN6	34 A3		Wilson Rd NN10	32 D3		Wellingborough NN8	24 B
Twyford Av NN8	23 H3		Warminster Cl NN18	6 A5		West St, Raunds NN9	21 G3		Wilson Ter NN16	14 C4		York Rd, Wollaston NN29	35 F
Tymecrosse Gdns LE16	4 B3		Warmonds Hill NN10	33 E4		West St, Rushden NN10	33 E3		Wilson Way NN6	34 B4		York St LE16	5 D
Tynan Cl NN15	17 G2		Warren Cl NN29	31 H6		West St, Stanwick NN9	20 B6		Wilton Cl NN14	12 C3		Yorke Cl NN9	21 F
Tyne Cl NN8	23 F5		Warren Rd NN14	11 B4		West St,			Wilton Rd NN15	17 G2		Yorke Cl NN9	22 B
Tyne Rd NN17	6 C3		Warth Park Way NN9	21 E2		Wellingborough NN8	29 H1		Wimborne Walk NN18	6 A5			
Tyson Courtyard NN18	10 C4		Wartnaby St LE16	5 B5		West Villa Rd NN8	29 H1		Wimpole Cl NN9	29 F1			
			Warwick Av NN14	11 B5		West Way,			Wincanton Ct NN16	6 A6			
Uist Walk*,			Warwick Grn*,			Kettering NN15	13 D5		Winchester Rd NN10	33 G4			
Shetland Way NN17	6 B3		Market Harborough LE16	4 D4		West Way,			Windermere Dr,				
Ullswater Cl,			Warwick Rd,			Northampton NN6	34 A3		Rushden NN10	27 F3			
Rushden NN10	27 E3		Wellingborough NN9	21 G3		Westbrook NN8	29 E1		Windermere Dr,				
Ullswater Cl,			Warwick Rd NN8	30 A3		Westbury Walk*,			Wellingborough NN8	23 E6			
Wellingborough NN8	23 E6		Warwick Way NN17	6 B6		Beanfield Av NN18	6 B6		Windermere Rd NN16	13 D4			
Ullswater Rd NN16	13 C3		Washbrook Rd NN8	32 D2		Westcott Way NN18	3 A3		Windmill Av,				
Underwood Rd NN14	19 A2		Washington Sq*,			Western Av LE16	5 B7		Kettering NN16	14 D5			
Union St,			Central Av NN16	3 C4		Western Cl NN18	29 F2		Windmill Av,				
Desborough NN14	12 D3		Water La, Corby NN17	10 E5		Westfield Av,			Wellingborough NN9	21 F4			
Union St, Kettering NN14	14 B4		Water La, Kettering NN16	11 D1		Rushden NN10	32 C3		Windmill Banks NN10	27 F4			
Union St,			Water Meadow Cl NN18	8 C5		Westfield Av,			Windmill Cl,				
Wellingborough NN9	22 C2		Water St NN16	14 D5		Wellingborough NN9	21 E5		Kettering NN16	11 D1			
Union Wharf LE16	4 B4		Waterfall Pl LE16	4 C3		Westfield Cl LE16	5 A6		Windmill Cl,				
Unity Cl NN29	35 F4		Waterhouse Gdns NN15	17 G3		Westfield Ct NN10	27 E6		Wellingborough NN9	29 H3			
Unity Cl NN14	12 C4		Waterloo Way NN8	26 B3		Westfield Dr NN16	32 C3		Windmill Cl,				
Unity St NN14	12 C4		Waterloo Yd NN8	30 A1		Westfield Rd NN8	29 G1		Wollaston NN29	35 G5			
Upper Dane NN10	27 F4		Watermill Cl NN14	12 F3		Westfields Av NN16	27 E6		Windmill Gro NN9	21 G2			
Upper George St NN16	27 F4		Waterworks La NN8	23 G4		Westfields St NN10	27 E6		Windmill La NN9	21 F2			
Upper Green Pl LE16	4 C2		Watson Av LE16	5 A8		Westfields Ter NN16	27 F6		Windmill Rd,				
Upper Havelock St NN8	24 A6					Westhill Cl NN15	13 D4		Rushden NN10	32 D3			
Upper Kings Av NN10	27 F4					Westhill Dr NN15	13 D5		Windmill Rd,				
Upper Park Av NN10	32 D4					Westleigh Rd NN15	17 H2		Wellingborough NN9	36 A5			
Upper Queen St NN10	32 D4								Windmill Rise NN16	11 D1			
Upper St NN16	14 B5								Windsor Av NN14	12 B4			
Upper Steeping NN14	12 D4												